Current

CONTROVERSIES

The Gig Economy

Other Books in the Current Controversies Series

The Gig Economy

Bridey Heing, Book Editor

GREENHAVEN
PUBLISHING

Published in 2021 by Greenhaven Publishing, LLC
353 3rd Avenue, Suite 255, New York, NY 10010

Library of Congress Cataloging-in-Publication Data

Names: Heing, Bridey, editor.
Title: The gig economy / Bridey Heing, book editor.
Description: First edition. | New York, NY : Greenhaven Publishing, 2021. |
  Series: Current controversies | Includes bibliographical references and
  index. | Audience: Grades 9–12.
Identifiers: LCCN 2020003150 | ISBN 9781534507067 (library binding) | ISBN
  9781534507050 (paperback)
Subjects: LCSH: Temporary employment—United States—Juvenile literature. |
  Part-time employment—United States—Juvenile literature. | Labor
  market—United States—Juvenile literature.
Classification: LCC HD5854.2.U6 G55 2021 | DDC 331.25/7290973—dc23
LC record available at https://lccn.loc.gov/2020003150

Manufactured in the United States of America

Website: http://greenhavenpublishing.com

Contents

Chapter 1: Is the Gig Economy a Positive Innovation for Workers and Consumers?

Western Governors University

Like any facet of the economy, the growing gig economy is complex. Determining the pros and cons of this emerging phenomenon highlights the ways in which workers and employers interact with it.

Yes: Overall, the Gig Economy Is a Beneficial Innovation

Aditya Gupta

Despite growing pains and a need for regulation, the gig economy is a response to our current economic situation and one that is remaking the way we think about work.

International Labour Organization (ILO)

The gig economy presents challenges, but with proper oversight and reform, the gig economy can be a positive force for workers.

Mark Stabile

According to recent research, being self-employed in the gig economy can help boost workers' sense of self-worth and happiness, resulting in positive mental health impacts.

No: The Gig Economy Is Dangerous for Workers and the Future of Work

Chapter 2: Does the Gig Economy Fill a Need in the Labor Market?

**Yes: The Gig Economy Provides Opportunities
for a Changing Workforce**

Chapter 3: Should the Gig Economy Be More Regulated?

Yes: The Gig Economy Needs to Be Regulated to Protect Workers and Consumers from Predatory Companies

Foreword

C ontroversy" is a word that has an undeniably unpleasant connotation. It carries a definite negative charge. Controversy can spoil family gatherings, spread a chill around classroom and campus discussion, inflame public discourse, open raw civic wounds, and lead to the ouster of public officials. We often feel that controversy is almost akin to bad manners, a rude and shocking eruption of that which must not be spoken or thought of in polite, tightly guarded society. To avoid controversy, to quell controversy, is often seen as a public good, a victory for etiquette, perhaps even a moral or ethical imperative.

Yet the studious, deliberate avoidance of controversy is also a whitewashing, a denial, a death threat to democracy. It is a false sterilizing and sanitizing and superficial ordering of the messy, ragged, chaotic, at times ugly processes by which a healthy democracy identifies and confronts challenges, engages in passionate debate about appropriate approaches and solutions, and arrives at something like a consensus and a broadly accepted and supported way forward. Controversy is the megaphone, the speaker's corner, the public square through which the citizenry finds and uses its voice. Controversy is the life's blood of our democracy and absolutely essential to the vibrant health of our society.

Our present age is certainly no stranger to controversy. We are consumed by fierce debates about technology, privacy, political correctness, poverty, violence, crime and policing, guns, immigration, civil and human rights, terrorism, militarism, environmental protection, and gender and racial equality. Loudly competing voices are raised every day, shouting opposing opinions, putting forth competing agendas, and summoning starkly different visions of a utopian or dystopian future. Often these voices attempt to shout the others down; there is precious little listening and considering among the cacophonous din. Yet listening and considering, too, are essential to the health of a democracy. If controversy is democracy's lusty lifeblood, respectful listening and careful thought are its higher faculties, its brain, its conscience.

Current Controversies does not shy away from or attempt to hush the loudly competing voices. It seeks to provide readers with as wide and representative as possible a range of articulate voices on any given controversy of the day, separates each one out to allow it to be heard clearly and fairly, and encourages careful listening to each of these well-crafted, thoughtfully expressed opinions, supplied by some of today's leading academics, thinkers, analysts, politicians, policy makers, economists, activists, change agents, and advocates. Only after listening to a wide range of opinions on an issue, evaluating the strengths and weaknesses of each argument, assessing how well the facts and available evidence mesh with the stated opinions and conclusions, and thoughtfully and critically examining one's own beliefs and conscience can the reader begin to arrive at his or her own conclusions and articulate his or her own stance on the spotlighted controversy.

This process is facilitated and supported in each Current Controversies volume by an introduction and chapter overviews that provide readers with the essential context they need to begin engaging with the spotlighted controversies, with the debates surrounding them, and with their own perhaps shifting or nascent opinions on them. Chapters are organized around several key questions that are answered with diverse opinions representing all points on the political spectrum. In its content, organization, and methodology, readers are encouraged to determine the authors' point of view and purpose, interrogate and analyze the various arguments and their rhetoric and structure, evaluate the arguments' strengths and weaknesses, test their claims against available facts and evidence, judge the validity of the reasoning, and bring into clearer, sharper focus the reader's own beliefs and conclusions and how they may differ from or align with those in the collection or those of classmates.

Research has shown that reading comprehension skills improve dramatically when students are provided with compelling, intriguing, and relevant "discussable" texts. The subject matter of these collections could not be more compelling, intriguing, or urgently relevant to today's students and the world they are poised to inherit. The anthologized articles also provide the basis for stimulating, lively, and passionate classroom debates. Students who are compelled to anticipate objections to their own argument and identify the flaws in those of an opponent read more carefully, think more critically, and steep themselves in relevant context, facts, and information more thoroughly. In short, using discussable text of the kind provided by every single volume in the Current Controversies series encourages close reading, facilitates reading comprehension, fosters research, strengthens critical thinking, and greatly enlivens and energizes classroom discussion and participation. The entire learning process is deepened, extended, and strengthened.

If we are to foster a knowledgeable, responsible, active, and engaged citizenry, we must provide readers with the intellectual, interpretive, and critical-thinking tools and experience necessary to make sense of the world around them and of the all-important debates and arguments that inform it. We must encourage them not to run away from or attempt to quell controversy but to embrace it in a responsible, conscientious, and thoughtful way, to sharpen and strengthen their own informed opinions by listening to and critically analyzing those of others. This series encourages respectful engagement with and analysis of current controversies and competing opinions and fosters a resulting increase in the strength and rigor of one's own opinions and stances. As such, it helps readers assume their rightful place in the public square and provides them with the skills necessary to uphold their awesome responsibility—guaranteeing the continued and future health of a vital, vibrant, and free democracy.

Introduction

> *"The gig economy is empowerment.*
> *This new business paradigm*
> *empowers individuals to better shape*
> *their own destiny and leverage their*
> *existing assets to their benefit."*
>
> *-John McAfee, computer*
> *programmer and businessman*

The way we work plays a crucial role in the way we live our lives and the way society functions. Traditionally, jobs have been a source of stability, benefits, and wages that for many people facilitated a middle class lifestyle. But in the past twenty years, an increase in demand for skilled labor, the recession of 2007-2008, and the rise of tech have facilitated a shift in how people are employed. Contract positions, rather than full employment, are becoming a new norm.

Today, the Federal Reserve estimates that around seventy-five million people are employed in what has become known as the gig economy.[1] The gig economy is a broad umbrella term that encompasses anyone who works full- or part-time in a position in which they are not considered an employee of the company they work for. Instead, they work "gigs," or one-off jobs, and they receive a set amount of money for completing this work. The government considers babysitters, ride-share drivers, and unofficial delivery people through apps like Postmates to be gig workers, along with others.

"Gig" employment isn't new in and of itself; the term "gig" is most often associated with the arts—for instance, a musician who is playing a show might refer to it as a gig. But the gig economy has grown so significantly in recent years that the public and the government are beginning to reconsider the purpose and ethics of companies that have thrived on gig labor. While many experts often speak of the ways in which gig work has disrupted the traditional economy, many others also discuss the impact of erratic and often low-paid work on the economy and well-being of those working such jobs.

Working in the gig economy can take many forms, and there is no set definition of who is and is not participating in it beyond the idea that employees who receive benefits or have their income taxed as W-2 income (meaning the employer withholds taxes from their paycheck) are not part of this population. However, some gig workers have full- or part-time regular work in addition to their work in the gig economy. Most gig work is associated with the rise of apps through which they can take one-off jobs, whether that's cleaning a house, picking up people through a rideshare app, or delivering takeout. The amount of money earned by the worker is determined by how many tasks they complete—how many rides they pick up and how long those rides are, how many homes they clean, or how many takeout orders they deliver, for example. The worker receives no benefits through the company, including health insurance and retirement. Additionally, the company often doesn't assume any liability for injury on the job, meaning that the worker has little to no recourse if they are hurt and are unable to work. The worker is also responsible for paying their own taxes and Social Security, as the company does not withhold taxes from each paycheck.

The benefits of this kind of work include flexible scheduling and the ability to choose which assignments one wants. The worker is also not obligated to work; if they do not want to or cannot work, they can simply choose not to do so and will not receive any punishment or be fired as a result. These jobs have become increasingly popular as a side job for those who want to make extra money in addition to their regular job and those who work in other unstable professions with unfixed hours. But as the gig economy grows and questions of regulation grow with it, many are uncertain whether these jobs offer much freedom at all or are instead exploiting people who are desperate to make ends meet.

In the viewpoints presented in *Current Controversies: The Gig Economy*, readers will be exposed to a range of perspectives and ideas about the gig economy, the role it is playing in the wider economy, and how workers within it can be protected. Readers will gain an understanding of a growing economic phenomenon—one driven by companies they will likely recognize—and deepen their understanding of the dynamic market in which they live and will someday work.

Notes

1. Elisabeth Buchwald, "The government has no idea how many gig workers there are, and that's a problem," *MarketWatch,* January 7, 2019, https://www.marketwatch.com/story/the-government-has-no-idea-how-many-gig-workers-there-areheres-why-thats-a-problem-2018-07-18.

CHAPTER1

Is the Gig Economy a Positive Innovation for Workers and Consumers?

The Gig Economy Presents Opportunities and Disadvantages

Western Governors University

Western Governors University is a private, career-focused online university based in Salt Lake City, Utah.

You may have heard different studies or information on the "gig economy" and wondered what exactly they are talking about. The gig economy isn't as confusing as it may seem. It's simply the idea that a diverse group of people with differing vocational skills are earning their money in a similar way. Another way to put it is freelance or contract work. Workers in the gig economy make money by matching with individual clients and completing work, or "gigs" for those clients to earn their money. Some gigs are as short as a five-minute survey, others are month or year-long projects. Regardless of how long the gig is, workers who earn their income through the gig economy must have a next project once their current one is done.

Size and Projections on Growth

It can be extremely difficult to determine exactly how many working adults are participating in the gig economy. According to Nation 1099 and information from the Bureau of Labor Statistics, roughly 11% of US workers are getting their full-time income from the gig economy. The data also suggests that many more people are participating in the gig economy with "side hustles" or other types of part-time or occasional freelance work.

Pros for Workers

There are a variety of pros to being a freelancer in the gig economy:

"The pros and cons of the gig economy," Western Governors University, August 31, 2018. Reprinted by permission.

Flexibility

Many freelance workers in the gig economy find that their status allows them great flexibility. From working the hours they desire, to working where they want, there are many options for gig economy workers. Often a task will be given to a worker with an end date, and how and when they accomplish that task is up to them. Often workers are able to work at hours that suit them and their needs and on days that work for them. Some may find that early mornings on the weekends are the ideal time to get their work done, and that may not be an option with a traditional job. Workers are often given the flexibility to work from a remote office or from home. This is often attractive to people who are trying to work around family schedules.

Greater Independence

Many contract or gig economy workers find that they are given independence to complete their work. Not being in an office may aid this independence. With nobody to look over shoulders, gig economy workers may find they are given a task and then mostly left alone to complete it. This can be a great boost of confidence and give workers the ability to complete a job the way they believe it will be best done—on their timetable and in their way.

A Variety of Jobs

Gig economy workers may find they have a wide variety of jobs to complete. Instead of similar, monotonous tasks to be done each day, each project or gig may be filled with different elements that make the work interesting. Workers may then find that they are more excited about projects and able to be more creative with their work because it varies each day.

Pay

Pay for freelance workers is variable from company to company. Some companies pay gig workers less, while many pay their workers more because they aren't having to pay benefits in addition to salary. Often they are able to charge hourly rates for their time.

This means they are able to control their work hours and get paid for extra hours on the clock. Things like meetings and phone calls in addition to regular work are billable. Obtaining higher education while working in a gig economy job is possible because both are extremely flexible. Adding another degree to your resume can potentially help you earn more money, as a freelancer or as a full-time employee.

Many gig economy workers may find that an online degree is an ideal way for them to get the education needed to be qualified for freelance jobs. Online degrees from WGU have similar pros when it comes to flexibility and independence, which may appeal to those who want to end up working in a gig economy job.

Cons for Workers

While there are quite a few pros to gig economy jobs, there are also downsides that make it difficult:

No Benefits

Unfortunately, for most gig economy jobs, benefits aren't part of the package. Because you're not a full-time employee of the organization, the laws regarding the benefits the company needs to give you are different. Some businesses will offer benefits to longer-term contractors, but this is rare. Gig economy workers should plan on budgeting for purchasing private insurance. They also need to plan retirement and budget how much of a paycheck to put towards that each month. From IRAs to 401ks, there are many options for how to save money for retirement. Most businesses will not handle this for freelance workers, so it's best to talk to a financial advisor and find out what the options are and which is best for each individual situation.

Quarterly Taxes, Personal Expenses

Similarly, most companies won't remove taxes from your paycheck for you. That means paying taxes is something you'll have to plan for. The IRS allows you to pay quarterly tax payments based on what you've earned. Most freelancers should plan on paying 25-

30 percent of each of their paychecks for taxes in order to not owe the IRS come tax time. These tax payments can simply be a check mailed to the IRS with the proper paperwork.

Gig economy workers are also usually responsible for personal expenses associated with working, like laptops and cell phones. While these can be written off for taxes, it's important to be careful with what you deduct. Many freelancers find it best to work with an accountant so they can go over all the things they use for their work, and know what to write-off for their taxes.

Isolation, Lack of Cultural Solidarity

Some workers may find the remote, removed life of the gig economy a problem. Often freelance workers don't go into the office and miss on the social elements present there. From parties to regular watercooler talks, gig economy workers may find they spend their day alone, working from home or from a remote site. While this adds flexibility, it can also cause isolation from the other workers and the feeling of being removed or left out.

More Stress

Gig economy workers have to regularly be working to find their next gig, or be prepared for changes in their current one. This can lead to stress, as most people appreciate feeling secure and steady in their employment. Gig economy workers sometimes face unexpected changes in their jobs, from being let go, to a change in their salary. There is also stress in being removed from other employees and if there are questions or issues with a project, that can be difficult to communicate.

Pros for Businesses

Lower Cost

Because companies don't have to pay for benefits or the onboarding costs of a full-time, new employee, freelance workers often have a lower cost than other workers. Employers are able to pay a salary and sometimes don't even have to provide work equipment for gig economy workers. This allows them to cut costs and just pay for the actual labor that a freelancer gives.

Ability to Scale Quickly
Many smaller or startup companies find freelance workers allow them to quickly scale their company. Without the need to provide office space, equipment, and benefits, small companies simply need to find people who have their own computer and are able to do the work. These workers can be found fast and with little marketing, sometimes through word of mouth. Then companies are able to meet goals and demands of their market while still keeping their costs low. They are able to save time and money setting up healthcare or HR programs and can simply hire workers to do simple projects that need to be done at the time.

Diverse Pool of Flexible Workers
Utilizing gig economy workers allows businesses to have a diverse pool of flexible workers at their disposal. These workers often work different hours from normal business hours, so needing something done late at night or early in the morning is less difficult. Workers are also often willing to do some weekend work, since they can do it from home, giving businesses options and flexibility. Gig economy workers are often various ages and skill levels, and businesses can utilize workers for different projects based on their skills. The often varying backgrounds gig economy workers bring to the table can actually allow for more creativity and ideas for the company.

Cons for Businesses
Less Reliable Workers
Sometimes, gig economy workers are looking for remote jobs because they aren't willing to work as hard. This is unfortunate for businesses, and they should be thorough in setting up expectations and in selecting freelance workers to ensure they will have a reliable employee.

Tight Regulations on Contractor Status

Businesses interested in hiring freelance workers need to understand all the regulations for contractor status in their state. Some states require written agreements, others are "at-will" statements, meaning either employee or employer can end the relationship at any time. There is often paperwork that needs to be filed and income information that is different from regular, full-time employees that needs to be given for taxes. This can be a bit of headache for businesses to navigate.

Workers in the gig economy are vital to the ever-changing landscape of the corporate world. While there are both pros and cons to freelance workers, all sides can agree that gig economy careers are continuing to impact businesses.

The Gig Economy Is the Latest Wave of Economic Innovation

Aditya Gupta

Aditya Gupta is the cofounder of Team iGenero, a digital marketing solutions manager based in Hyderabad, India.

L ying on the couch, I'm working on my laptop. A few minutes later, I find myself scrolling through the infinite food options on Swiggy. You've probably used one of the many "food-tech" apps either to search for a restaurant, make a reservation at your favourite bar. Restaurant picked, the discount code applied & order placed! The delivery guy soon arrives. He is the human link in a technology-driven industry of convenience. He has several counterparts—those who drive you back from a late night party to the ones who bring you groceries or those who lend you their home for your trip—living the courier lifestyle.

Welcome to the Gig Economy where an army of workers called "giggers" are creating their own destiny as companies like Uber, AirBnb, Ola, Zomato, Swiggy and others are using technology to disrupt industries. This shift claims to focus on the worker where one gets to choose his/her own work hours in a hi-tech frontier, departing from the usual 9 to 5 jobs!

The term "gig economy" was first coined by journalist Tina Brown in 2009. She wrote about the trend of workers pursuing "a bunch of free-floating projects, consultancies and part-time bits and pieces while they transacted in a digital marketplace." To sum up, Gigs are either skill-based assignments or need-based tasks.

As they say, there's nothing new under the Sun. The same holds true to the Gig Economy which perhaps existed from ancient days where a man decided to hunt and gather. And, the formula is similar: *Go out, explore, learn more!* Interestingly, the full-time

"Gig Economy & The Future Of Work," by Aditya Gupta, Team iGenero, July 3, 2019. Reprinted by permission.

employment culture, which has redefined what a traditional job looks like, is also a fairly recent phenomenon.

Where It All Began

Prior to the industrial revolution and until the Victorian era, people worked multiple jobs to piece together a decent living. The Gig Economy of unpredictable employment patterns sprang up when industrial jobs were seasonal. Historian (at Cornell University) Louis Hyman's years of research revealed that companies like Manpower Inc. and Kelly Girl provided temporary labour (mostly women secretaries) to big corporations to bridge gaps in the workforce.

"The industrial revolution was preceded by the industrious revolution, a social reorganisation of people, which involved groups working together in small spaces, dividing up tasks so that each labourer didn't have to be as skilled" Hyman explains.

As the noise for better employee welfare and benefits got shriller and louder from trade unions between the 1930 and 1950s, a tremendous shift in larger corporations' attitude towards employees was evident. With legal systems in place following the labour movement, corporations began prioritising employee benefits such as social security, medical leaves and paid leaves, unemployment insurance, health insurance, pensions, life insurance, etc.

Economic Downturns Fuel Gigs

Piece-work has long been part of middle-income workers ever since the industrial revolution. Part-time work witnessed a spike world over from the 1980s when traditional organisations began moving away from full-time employment offers towards short-term, more flexible staffing opportunities. This was a result of lean revolution to cut costs and focus on short-term profits. In the following decade, agencies for temporary workers spouted where 85% of the companies began using temporary labour by decreasing employee benefits.

Gigs generally seem hot in a recession which was exactly what happened during the 1991 economic downturn. As a result of job losses, alternative work began gaining ground as a response to the weak labour market. A few years later, the Internet's evolution in 1995 and the inception of Craigslist in the consecutive year—all seemed to work wonders in boosting the prospects of the alternative workforce.

Between 1995 and 2005, the number of workers with alternative employment arrangements for their main job went up from 12.1 million workers to 14.8 million in 2005 in the US, according to the Bureau of Labour Statistics.

The fad of fast-growing subset of gigs continued to awe people while Amazon became one of the first companies to jump onto the Gig Economy bandwagon in 2005. But the following years leading to the Great Recession in 2008 made life difficult as money was tight and jobs were scarce. People looked for ways to supplement their stagnant wages and dwindling savings. This pent-up demand was met with a new type of work that enabled the gig economy. Simultaneously, companies began shifting from antiquated full-time workforce model to contract-based (on-demand) workers.

Tech-Driven Industry of Convenience

Interestingly, the period of recession saw giggers crowding the customer service segment of work. The inclusion of a flexible workforce eventually opened up organisations to the idea of being more agile and accommodative. What changed was that 70% of employers in the developed countries truly believed that giggers increased their profitability and efficiency.

On the other hand, the app-based economy has also made us (consumers) smarter, better connected and more demanding as we love the speed and convenience that the digital platforms offer. Not only has this enabled in consolidating remote and mobile workers by directly connecting service providers to customers but also made consumers' voice more powerful.

Though there is no accurate estimate of their numbers, it is projected that this "flex" or "mobile economy" will comprise half the workforce by 2020, and as much as 80% by 2030. Gig Economy is symbolic of the kind of contract work expanding into every corner of the economy—more like the reincarnation of contract work.

A McKinsey study estimates that 20–30% of the workforce in developed countries already engages in some form of independent work. Adding to this, India is home to the second largest market of freelance professionals (about 15 million), standing next only to the US (nearly 53 million). Most of them have full-time roles but also work side-hustles which they earn from. These 15 million Indian freelancers contribute to about 40% of total freelance jobs offered worldwide, a report by ICRIER states.

The proliferation of apps such as Uber, Lyft, AirBnB, TaskRabbit and others have defined the direction of today's global economy by disrupting sclerotic industries which do not adapt easily. However, all is not hunky dory in this fluid workforce.

It's Not All Sunshine and Rainbows in Gig Life

The Gig life comes with many riders. In fact, several companies supporting the Gig Economy have been blatantly accused of exploiting their workers as there is no safety net for giggers who are part of the ecosystem. In the process, their rights and pay is compromised. Gig life also means that there are no standard benefits such as pensions, hikes, sick pay, leaves or holiday entitlement.

Since most of the low-skilled gig workers are poorly paid and earn only based on the number of working hours clocked, financial insecurity also looms large. With this impending threat, they often give up their social life to overwork and make ends meet.

With payouts not guaranteed and gig work not being long-term, they find it difficult to get a bank loan or mortgage. Apart from this, they also have to pay taxes and file returns, irrespective of their wages. Some gigs, specifically, require licenses and permissions, depending on the region they are operating in, making it even more difficult and less reliable in the long-term.

For instance: Uber drivers can't really decide where they work. They are constantly nudged towards locations where the app wants them to be. And, if they want to make more money, they cannot be choosy about their working hours. The idea of this new boss—an algorithm—is different and more complex in the Gig Economy as we have traded human bosses to AI.

Meanwhile, workers also need to find their own gigs which can be a cumbersome process as it isn't easy unless you have an established relationship with a client. With no benchmarking system for freelance work, a gigger is often accused of overpricing projects or succumbs to ridiculous price bargains. Geographic flexibility in the gig economy also means more competition which in turn means lower bids for the same work. As a gig becomes popular, earning potential will always decrease. And, as earnings decrease, workers are forced to adjust their schedules to maximize their income.

Though the gig economy has helped workers leverage their skills, knowledge, and networks, it has shrunk the corporate resource pool by creating higher attrition rates among organisations. It also calls for the regular implementation of new technology platforms to manage churn faster. This can be very time consuming and costly.

But There Are Advantages to Being a Gigger

Companies supporting the sharing economy have helped create a novel form of business model where workers have a chance to earn money on their own schedules either through in-app payments and ratings-based marketplace ecosystem or by showcasing their expertise on tech platforms like UpWork, Fiver, PeoplePerHour, etc. They can either be freelancers or full-time workers with side-hustles or those on temporary contracts.

According to a report by Noble House titled, *The Future of Work is Anywhere—Gig Workforce*, 70% of the Indian Corporates have used gig workers at least once for major organisational issues in 2018. Further, the report said, nearly 45% of the human resource heads surveyed want to hire gig workers so that they can supplement the skills of the existing workforce and 39% would do this to reduce the cost and 10% for filling temporary vacancies in their teams.

As bigger corporations are willing to experiment with temporary workers, they can save costs as employee training and employee protection expenditure go down drastically and scale up quickly. In this model, gig workers get personal time as they choose their own work hours which allows them to network and improve productivity.

The free will also helps them decide the price on their projects and, at a time and place of their choice. They also have the advantage of finding a variety of jobs and being at their creative best as every project could be different. Obtaining higher education or learning new skills is possible for gig workers, given the flexibility of time and work. Sometimes, gig workers earn more than full-time employees as pay varies from client to client.

In fact, several studies show that people with more control over their schedules and flexibility in choosing their work are significantly more satisfied with their work than their peers who hold regular salaried jobs, despite losing out on benefits and security. For a clear majority, it is a conscious decision to embrace the gig economy.

Companies Supporting Mobile Economy

The companies enabling the gig economy are essentially replacing contracting companies. For instance: If there's a wedding and I'm looking for manpower, there an app for supplying the manpower. Similarly, if I'm making an ad film and am looking for background actors, I could as well use an app to hire them than to approach a talent agency. More importantly, these platforms are powerful enough to serve your demand real-time. I don't need to book a ticket in advance nor do I need to book a cab hours before my schedule anymore. Everything's available on my fingertips!

Upwork is another platform that offers gigs from low to high level skill set, seeks to connect businesses to a reliable and larger pool of quality talent, while workers simultaneously can enjoy freedom and flexibility to find jobs online. Another example is that of "Flexing It." It has a network of over 50,000 freelancers and 19,000 clients and it aims to create a market for specialised, experienced independent consultants in India. So, if you are looking for highly skilled consultants ranging from senior associates to experienced directors and strategy consultants, then this is the place to be!

Similarly, Uber's disruption of the taxicab industry, based largely on identifying opportunities for innovation in transporting people, has democratised workspace globally. And, now product companies such as Zomato, Swiggy, Food Panda, UberEats, UrbanClap, HouseJoy have all followed the same model, contributing to the Gig Economy.

Growing Pangs of Unrest

Despite the convenience of being able to open an app, book a cab and jump into it, the global expansion of gig work has caused friction and controversy. In November 2018, Uber and Ola drivers went on a strike to protest against the fall in their earnings and a similar strike was carried out by Swiggy delivery executives in December 2018. These workers are not represented by any trade unions and are generally considered to be self-employed. Going by that logic, some platforms like Swiggy, Zomato and Uber Eats which claim to be neutral, mandate their delivery executives to wear a uniform, indicating how their workers must do their duty of acting like employees.

With app-based tech aggregators facing such repeated challenges over the demands of employee benefits from gig workers, the threat of automation always plagues them as it is seen as the future of businesses. Moreover, autonomous vehicles or driverless cars are likely to prove much safer than conventional ones, they believe. Similarly, e-commerce giants are experimenting with drone delivery which eliminates the hassles of navigating through traffic snarls or relying heavily on human resources.

A Dire Need for Regulation

Even as a sizeable chunk of workers remain outside the traditional employment structure, there is a dire need for regulations or policies which create a safety net for workers in the sharing economy. When it comes to managing the on-demand workforce, many organizations suffer from fragmented governance models and manual processes.

Currently, one proposal being floated is to create a third category of worker, sitting somewhere between self-employed and employed—the *independent worker*. This classification bridges the gap between traditional employees and contractors, acknowledging the unique characteristics of independent workers and giving them the right to bargain for protection from employment discrimination.

Europe and Britain already have introduced legislation which gives more leverage and power to gig workers in choosing predictable hours of work along with benefits of leaves to put an end to "abusive practices" around casual contracts.

In India, the gig economy is at a nascent stage but is growing rapidly. According to a Millennial Survey by Deloitte, 16.8% of millennials evaluate career opportunities by good work-life balance, followed by 13.4% who look for opportunities to progress, and 11% who seek flexibility. This is one of the main reasons why millennials are attracted to the gig economy.

Not falling behind, the Indian Government in 2015 introduced a freelance scheme under its Digital India platform. While it has recognised gig workers and entrepreneurs, the rules are still fuzzy. Since there is no proposal for a regulation protecting gig workers in India, benefits such as overtime pay, paid or sick leave, health or medical allowance, protection from harassment or discrimination among gig workers are still not recognised.

However, the Indian government could model a policy for gig economy around innovations such as Australia's GigSuper, a fund which makes it easier for gig workers to save for a pension. Given that workers in the gig economy are vital to the ever-changing landscape of the corporate world, insisting that these gig platforms follow the rules laid by the government would give workers greater protection while ensuring that the gig economy lives up to its enormous promise.

A Full-Time Reality

As the current workforce's obsession with freedom intensifies, the gig economy will continue to grow and disrupt businesses. The Gig Economy's digital platforms consistently deliver choice, control and options for people who choose to build portfolio careers. Those who are not reliant on gig work, use it for supplemental income while those who are charmed by its flexibility and pay are seeing it as the best overall option.

Within the next five years, it is predicted that the global workforce will comprise nearly 50% independent contractors. This is both a blessing and disguise, especially for younger people entering the workforce. In the past, even those without a career path would end up falling into a nice profession by simply following a standard track. But faced with the ever-changing face of work in a tech-driven world, one needs to be more skill-oriented and driven at least to make it to the first of the many professional ladders. So, we need to make investments in our infrastructure and make changes to the way we take care of workers.

Additionally, app-based businesses will become an important part of the world's economy, compelling traditional ones to adapt an app-based labour market in ways we cannot yet anticipate. Maybe, your job of the future will be a gig and you may be getting more freedom from your employer through an app, a technology or a robot! But for now, the Gig Economy is here to stay and has a long way to go before side hustles become a full-time reality!

There Are Ways to Make the Gig Economy Work for Employees

International Labour Organization (ILO)

The ILO is a United Nations agency that works to set international labor standards and advance social justice around the world.

The gig economy has received enormous public attention over the past few years. But how can workers in the platform economy have their interests represented and bargain for better pay and working conditions?

Over the last few years, the development of newer technologies has brought fundamental changes to the way we work and the type of locations at which we do that work. Standard work contracts and engagement with an employer have changed dramatically which seems to be making work more intermittent and in many cases less stable.

This is due in part to long-term trends of non-standard work arrangements, and the rise of the platform economy or gig economy which has become a major game-changer.

Companies that are part of the gig economy are on the verge of overtaking the traditional economy. A driver, a musician, a freelance videographer or anything in between, the concept has caught on and is a major factor in how sectors are organised and how people view work. And while one-off jobs are not new, the increasing use of technology has substantially contributed to a wide proliferation of "gig" work.

The gig economy has been growing exponentially in size and importance in recent years and its impact on labour rights has been largely overlooked. It is still difficult to estimate the exact number of workers, as businesses are sometimes reluctant to disclose the data. It is rather complicated to draw an estimate, since workers might be registered with more companies in the same month, week, or day.

However, available estimates range from 0.7 to 34 percent. The Bureau of Labor Statistics reported in 2017 that 55 million people in the US are "gig workers." This accounts for approximately 34 percent of the US workforce, projected to increase to 43 percent in 2020.

Getting paid for ones' work in the gig economy also seems to be a big problem. A recent survey by the New York-based Freelancers Union indicates that 50 percent of freelancers have trouble getting compensated for their work. Late payment was usually the problem, however a third of those surveyed experienced situations in which they were not paid at all for work already completed.

There is also a growing body of research that makes a useful distinction between "crowdwork" and "work on-demand via apps." For example crowdworkers operate online through platforms that connect vast numbers of clients, organizations, and businesses, often across borders. Because crowdwork is performed online, an infinite number of workers and clients are often spread over large geographic distances.

On the other hand, "work-on demand via apps," is platform-facilitated yet place-based and geographically limited work. These distinctions result in different strategies used by crowdworkers and place-based platform workers.

Are workers using the gig-economy to top up their income or is it their only income?

Informal conversations with people participating in the gig economy have provided different perspectives on the value of their new jobs in the gig economy. Some have said that it gets them out of the house or provides them with something to do or to meet new people. This reply was more common among retirees. Others said it helped them pay for a special night out or buy an extra bag of groceries. None of the respondents in these informal discussions said it paid a wage they could live on and hence they had to hold several side jobs to make ends meet.

The rise of the gig economy can pose risks to societies at-large, when for example it becomes the only economy, replacing entire groups of employees and their full-time jobs with workers who are not protected by labor laws, or eligible for benefits and social security. This new class of workers, who are constantly searching for new contracts, may not be able to keep up with the most important factor in the future of work: developing new skills.

In the gig economy, work has been broken down into smaller, time-bound tasks. This has given rise to an ever expanding universe of sites that list tasks for people to perform. These platforms include TaskRabbit, Upwork, FlexJobs, Uber, Rover, Fiverr, Care.com or Instacart which can often involve a simple service like hanging pictures or driving a car to more complex but equally short-term work such as Virtual Executive Assistants to Medical Auditors.

Consumers outsource services to gig workers because they do not have time to do it themselves or it is simply cheaper than hiring a company. While gig-workers are constantly in search for their next work assignments, it is difficult to engage in learning new skills. The types of skills needed in today's labour market have been changing rapidly and therefore individual workers need to engage in life-long learning to maximize their employment opportunities.

On the other side, companies realize that they have to plan reskilling strategies for their employees which must take a life-long learning approach. This can be an important approach for companies to attract and retain the best talent and be seen as a good employer that invests in talent and contributes to socially responsible business practices.

Today, many companies are helping educators to create skills-based programs and look to identify future job prospects at high schools, where talent can be discovered and nurtured early. This seems to be shifting some people's thinking about work and careers away from the traditional liberal-arts education which can prepare them for a college degree towards more job-related skills. This new approach aims to provide vocational skills to young people entering the labor force and set them up for better work prospects.

However, next to the technical skills, social skills and critical thinking will be of particular importance to future job-seekers. Additional qualities like creativity, empathy, communication, imagination, problem-solving or strategic thinking may become more important moving forward. The dilemma is that a traditional liberal arts education already provides these types of soft skills training so this component shouldn't be lost but rather supplemented by training on hard skills that are in demand.

In addressing today's persistent gap between the skills needed in the labour market and those offered by the workforce, the ILO recommends a skills anticipation or skills forecasting approach which is a strategic and systematic process through which labour market actors identify and prepare to meet future skills needs.

This helps to address the gaps between skills demand and supply. A skills anticipation strategy enables training providers, young people, policy-makers, employers and workers to make better educational and training choices, and through institutional mechanisms and information resources leads to improved use of skills and human capital development.

An important issue from the gig workers' side that is not often explored is the protection of their rights under labor law since the gig economy present unique challenges. Gig workers are often classified as independent contractors which under certain laws precludes them from forming associations to protect their rights and engaging in collective bargaining.

Gig workers often labour independently, in isolation, over geographically expansive areas, and in direct competition with one another. Additionally, gig work is often short term or task-based and online labour platforms have high worker turnover rates.

One thing is for certain, the gig economy will remain central to the future of work. The gig economy provides an important opportunity for income and employment for a growing number of workers. It enables workers who would normally be excluded from the labour market on account of disability, care responsibilities or illness, to participate.

However, there remains a number of concerns about the conditions of work, and the potential for the gig economy to provide consistent and fairly paid work for all who rely upon it. Smart and effective policies are needed to help both workers and the platforms live up to expectations.

The Gig Economy Can Have Beneficial Impacts on Workers' Mental Health

Mark Stabile

Mark Stabile is a professor of economics with INSEAD business school, which has campuses in Asia, the Middle East, and North America. He directs the James M. and Cathleen D. Stone Centre for the Study of Wealth Inequality.

The general picture of gig economy work and mental wellbeing is not a pretty one. Around the world, Uber drivers face wage and security worries. Deliveroo workers have too much competition. Airbnb owners face legal problems in Paris and other cities.

But while these headlines suggest a dark cloud over the heads of gig economy workers, recent data I've looked at unexpectedly shows that they are about 33% more likely to self-report positive mental health traits.

It may seem like a counterintuitive result but, in new research with Bénédicte Apouey, a professor at the Paris School of Economics, I found that self-employed gig economy workers in the UK score higher across a range of psychological wellbeing measures than workers in the mainstream economy.

Meanwhile, gig work in the UK is surging, with unemployment at a record low and demand rocketing for sharing-economy services. Deliveroo, for example, was named the UK's fastest growing tech firm for 2018 by Deloitte. Uber, although facing regulatory issues in the UK, still posted a huge increase in profit last year. Airbnb's market in London has increased fourfold since 2015.

"How gig economy work gives a mental health boost to workers—new research," by Mark Stabile, The Conversation, July 25, 2019, https://theconversation.com/how-gig-economy-gives-a-mental-health-boost-to-workers-new-research-120924. Licensed under CC BY-ND 4.0 International.

Self-Employment and Self-Worth

To find out how the gig economy is affecting people, we matched data from the Understanding Society study (the biggest long-term study of household attitudes in the UK) and Google Trends, which shows the popularity of different search terms at different times and places. Understanding Society has information about people's health and demographics, and tracks their employment type.

The Google search terms we analysed were primarily words associated with gig economy work in a given area. This served as a predictor for where people had gig employment at Uber, Deliveroo and Airbnb. Cross-referencing this data with the Understanding Society study, enabled us to analyse the mental health of people working in the gig economy.

We found that self-employed workers reported improved ability to concentrate and self-confidence, which are both important to mental health. These workers also reported a boost to self-worth and happiness.

The boost in self-confidence and concentration fits with benefits some workers in the sharing economy receive from not needing to adhere to certain restrictions found in traditional paid work, such as working schedules set by a boss or having long commutes. Other research indicates that Uber drivers in London, although they make less than most Londoners, have greater life satisfaction.

For employees in the mainstream economy, heavy job requirements plus low autonomy lead to stress. Employees with zero hours contracts—whose hours fluctuate from week to week but who lack control over their schedules—may be under even more stress than those with regular jobs. In contrast, gig workers decide when to work and make their own decisions about customers, leading to a greater sense of control.

Health Kick

Our health and wellbeing measures are from the General Health Questionnaire of the Understanding Society study, which evaluates the current state of mind of respondents and asks if it is different from their usual state. Some of the questions relate to concentration, loss of sleep due to worry, and feelings that they play a useful role or can face up to problems. Other questions ask if the subject is unhappy, depressed or lacking confidence.

The scores for our measures run from lowest mental health at 0 to the best psychological health at 36. The mean is around 24. We found that self-employment increases a subject's score by eight points—an improvement of roughly one third.

One very large change in the factors we examined was money spent on alcoholic drinks. For gig workers, it dropped by a breathtaking 200%. This isn't necessarily a reduction in consumption of alcohol, but in spending. Uber and Deliveroo drivers are often at work when people are down the pub or at meal times, when money is often spent on drink. These are peak hours for gig workers, who need to be sober on the job. It nonetheless results in a remarkable difference for mental health, especially in the UK, where alcohol misuse is the biggest factor for death and ill-health among those aged 15 to 49.

Our results also show that women, those without a university degree and older workers —groups that are often overlooked in the regular economy—fare particularly well in terms of mental health. The sharing economy offers not only flexibility but a direct connection that allows these workers to feel that they are making a real and immediate contribution.

For women especially, self-employment gives a level of flexibility to part-time work that isn't possible in the mainstream workforce. As women often bear the brunt of care responsibilities, this autonomy is vital to their mental health.

Lessons for All

Our preliminary conclusions point to the importance of autonomy in the workplace. The gig economy offers workers the opportunity for more control in their jobs, which may lead to more self-worth, more confidence, less strain.

It's clear that workers who have this control, as well as flexibility and the idea that they're making a difference, are more mentally healthy. Managers can weave flexibility into office life, empowering and engaging workers to be responsible for and confident in their decision making abilities.

Poor mental health is expensive for employers. In fact, it is estimated to cause 91m lost working days each year in the UK, costing the economy US$37.5 billion. This is, of course, not limited to the UK. In the US, it's estimated that US$193 billion in earnings is lost each year due to serious mental illness.

Past the dramatic articles about the perils of the gig economy, the changing nature of work needs more attention. Self-employment has a positive impact on mental health, even with some insecurity. In contrast, the precariousness of zero hours contracts, where workers often learn their schedule just a few days in advance, should not be associated with gains in wellbeing found among gig workers.

The Rise of the Gig Economy Has Opened Up Avenues of Exploitation

Julie Davies and Mark Horan

Julie Davies is an HR subject group leader at the University of Huddersfield in the United Kingdom. Mark Horan is a senior lecturer in human resource management at the University of Huddersfield.

Self-employment is on the rise in the UK. The latest government statistics put it at 4.79m, which represents 15% of all people in work. And, in recognition of this changing nature of employment, the prime minister has commissioned a review of workers' rights. One of its chief tasks is to address concerns that millions are stuck in insecure and stressful work.

Flexible working and self-employment are inevitable solutions to the growing "gig economy," in order to best manage projects and fluctuating work flows. A flexible lifestyle may be desirable for the highly paid IT consultant. But for the call centre worker on a zero-hours contract, it means a pension, mortgage and income protection are all illusory.

In Tim Ferriss' book *The 4-Hour Work Week*, creative freelancers live the dream. They work anywhere, anytime, provided they deliver agreed outputs. And, as social scientist Richard Florida suggests in his view of the "Creative Class," high-tech workers, artists and musicians typically gravitate to dynamic and open urban regions, with good schools, sporting and shopping facilities. These high-earning creative types then generate jobs for contingent workers whose rights must be protected from abuse. The challenge for urban planners is to attract such talent at both ends of the flexible working spectrum.

Flexibility in self-employment, however, presents a quite different scenario for those with zero-hours contracts. These are increasingly common employment contracts where employers do not guarantee the individual any work and the individual is not obliged to accept any work offered. They are a hot topic for debate, with significant polarisation of views.

The recent investigation into Sports Direct's use of zero-hours contracts showed them in a particularly negative light and there is talk of the company moving to fixed hours. New Zealand banned these types of contracts in April. And an employment tribunal in London recently ruled that Uber drivers should be classed as workers, rather than self-employed. Yet for some—students, for example—a zero-hours contract is better than no contract at all.

Despite the latest outrages over zero-hours contracts, theories of workplace flexibility have been around for many years. The academic John Atkinson put forward a well-known model for the "flexible firm" in 1984. It advocated that companies retain a core group of workers and use a flexible workforce that is determined by and responsive to business demand.

The model also distinguishes between functional and numerical flexibility. This has long been the operating model in the entertainment industry where the supply of staff is driven by business demand. It is a continuing theme in discussions about employment trends in the fourth industrial revolution.

A Business Staple

The high-profile coverage of zero-hours contracts might give the impression that they are one of the dominant forms of employment contract in the UK. But, government statistics show that 903,000 people were employed on them during April to June 2016—this is just 2.9% of all people in employment. They are most likely to be young, part-time, women, or in full-time education. Typically they work 25-hours per week and a third say they would prefer more hours in their current jobs.

Zero-hours contracts, however, are actually less prevalent than other forms of flexible and non-standard employment such as shift work, annualised hours and temporary contracts. And they are only slightly more common than agency work.

In effect, they can be seen as equivalent to the long-established position of a casual contract, something which has been the staple of the business model in the leisure, entertainment and culture industry for years. When work is seasonal, margins are narrow and covering the minimum wage is a challenge for employers, many of whom simply cannot afford surplus staff.

Juggling Act

One sector that experiences significant fluctuation in demand is the entertainment business. Blackpool, a seaside resort on the north-west English coast, whose main industry is tourism, is a good example of how difficult it is to get this right. There is a seasonal and school holiday cycle, which introduces one level of fluctuation. Then there are other unpredictable factors that affects the need for staff.

The famously variable British weather affects the relative popularity of indoor and outdoor attractions. And the city is host to a number of events, ranging from major darts competitions, musical acts and theatre productions, to small weddings and functions. The skills required varies significantly too. Whether it's the annual British Homing Pigeon World Show (January), the world ballroom dancing championships (May), or the annual Rebellion punk reunion festival (August). Flexibility is a daily challenge for many businesses in similar situations.

So, in a world of increasing flexibility and insecurity, we will watch with interest to see the outcome of the government's review of modern employment. Matthew Taylor who is running it has a wide remit that includes security, pay and rights; progression and training; finding the appropriate balance of rights and responsibilities for new models; representation; opportunities for under-represented groups; new business models. Taylor has said that "most part-time workers, and even most zero-hours workers, say they have chosen to work this way." Let's see whether the evidence really bears this out.

Rather Than Being Innovative, the Gig Economy Is Making Work Unsafe and Unstable

Anthony Gabb

Anthony Gabb is a professor of economics at St. John's University, New York. His research focuses on political economy and heterodox economics.

Uber, the embodiment of the sharing economy, was once again propelled into the spotlight on March 19, 2018, after one of its self-driving cars struck and killed a pedestrian in Arizona. This has resulted in renewed debate over the safety of Uber's driverless cars, as well as over its illegal and unethical tactics of skirting regulations, which are in part responsible for the company's rapid growth.

The gig economy is the future workplace, once associated with less industrialized countries in the 1970s, where temporary, unstable employment is commonplace and companies tend toward hiring employees who are all but in name performing the work of permanent workers but are denied permanent employee rights. It is glamorized by some, but the truth is, it undermines the traditional economy, and will aggravate unemployment, poverty and immigration. The "gigzombie" is the alienated gig employee whose vitality has been sapped by rapid technological advancements that are changing the nature of work and increasingly threatening job security.

Since the end of the post-WWII economic expansion in the 1970s, capitalism has been struggling with slow growth and flat wages. The gig economy, actuated by technological innovation, is a restructuring response to cut labor costs and increase profits. It is not a solution for unemployment, inequality and forced migration, yet estimates show that the gig economy will soon account for over 40 percent of the US workforce. Simultaneously, capitalism manufactures both wealth and

"The Uber Crash Is Just the Start: How the Gig Economy Threatens the Future of Work," by Anthony Gabb, Truthout, March 26, 2018. Reprinted by permission.

unemployment (thereby inequality and misery), which is necessary for its own existence. Immigrants are not the cause of unemployment, and the gig economy is not the solution.

Forces Giving Rise to the Gig Economy

To understand the need to restructure the future workplace to boost the corporate bottom line, it is important to understand the economic forces that have brought us to this point. As such, the Marxist theory of the accumulation of capital (wealth) assumes that "labor is the source of all value." The drive for profits gives rise to technological change. Labor and machines working together create more wealth.

The problem is that in order to create more wealth, workers are replaced by machines, which tend to cause more unemployment, torment and migration. As unemployed workers move into and out of the workforce, they are used as a lever to discipline the already employed by destroying unions, depressing wages, making it easy to lay off workers without notice and replacing them with temporary and part-time employees, destroying the social safety net, and keeping production costs down. When the number of displaced workers plus the increase in population is greater than the number of jobs created, the result is mass unemployment and poverty, which triggers migration to places where people think there are jobs. Immigration laws, which are anti-labor laws, are used to manage the ebb and flow of the global reserve army of the unemployed, by opening or closing the immigration spigot to make cheap labor available.

The point is that capitalism is unable to create dignified work with livable wages and benefits for everyone who wants to work. The system manufactures unemployment; it is a necessary outcome of the accumulation of wealth, and a tool used to perpetuate the existence of the system by pitting employed and unemployed workers, and US-born and immigrant workers against one other, making them compete for a limited number of jobs. As such, capitalism creates obscene levels of inequality; the rich get richer and the poor get poorer.

The Future Workplace

The workplace is rapidly transitioning from the traditional 40-hour workweek with benefits, to the gig economy, where there is a race to reduce labor cost, and at the same time, creating an environment where immigrants are an instrument of control due to the schism (the false notion that immigrants are taking our jobs) between them and the US-born workforce.

Technological innovations give employers the ability to identify, calculate and monitor how much employees produce wherever they are. In this increasingly automated workplace, digital technology enables employers to manage the workplace from afar, allowing them complete control over workers; the machine incorporates and absorbs the worker who is the appendage within it, and extracts wealth from it. Already, more than 34 percent of the workforce is employed as temporary part-time precarious employees and expected to soon grow to 43 percent of the total workforce.

The state plays a critical role in the transition to the gig economy by dismantling unions using "right-to-work" laws and re-writing tax laws that suggest people can get rich from becoming independent contractors. Under provisions of the Taft-Hartley Act that require unionized workplaces to become "open shops," employees must be allowed to work whether or not they join the union or pay dues. This makes it more difficult for workers to form unions. About 28 states in the US are right-to-work states. In part, right-to-work laws have devastated organized labor. Unionized workers on average are paid 27 percent more than non-union workers. If you want a raise, join a union is fast becoming a thing of the past. In the absence of union representation, labor costs decrease at the expense of workers, by reducing wages and benefits.

The recent tax law passed by Congress and signed by Trump gives $1.5 trillion to corporations and the wealthy. Some believe that tax cuts for small businesses offered by the new tax law will increase the pace to form independent contractor small businesses in order to take advantage of these tax cuts. This, however, comes at a cost, as employers shift the cost of wages and benefits—once hard-fought for by unions—onto employees.

The Future Workforce

As population grows and automation displaces millions of workers in farming and manufacturing, the levels of unemployment and the number of workers looking for work in the service sector increase. As the tendency toward mass unemployment and the transition from union to non-union, and full-time permanent status to temporary part-time independent contractors, consultants and freelancers increase, so too, has migration, the widening inequality gap and poverty.

The spectrum of the workforce, according to Marx, (the *proletariat*) spans from those who are working, to the mass unemployed (reserve army of the unemployed), to those who have lost their class identity—people who are very poor and disenfranchised (the *lumpen proletariat*). The actively employed are distributed among the primary, secondary and tertiary sectors. The reserve army of the unemployed includes the floating, latent and stagnant unemployed. During the last 40 years, while there has been an increase in the number of the actively employed, due to automation and an increase in the working-age portion of the global population, there has also been a significant increase in unemployment.

During this period, the number of workers displaced by automation, plus the increase in population has far outpaced the number of jobs created, both in the US and global economies. During the four decades beginning in 1977, from Presidents Carter to Obama, the US economy created 69.8 million jobs (Carter 10.5 million, Reagan 15.9 million, G.H.W. Bush 2.6 million, Clinton 21.5 million, G.W. Bush 2.1 million, and Obama 17.2 million)—an average of 1.7 million a year. The workforce grew an average of 1.6 million a year, and the number of yearly unemployed people ranged between 5.6 and 1.5 million. From 1980 to 2014, the number of people living in poverty in the US increased from 29.3 to 46.7 million. From 1990 to 2010, the size of the global workforce increased by 40 percent, or 1.3 billion people to 4.5 billion people.

The global industrial reserve army of the unemployed is projected to be 215 million, with only 40 million new jobs added; more than 60 percent of those who are employed are in precarious employment. By 2030, not accounting for population growth, an additional 400 to 800 million will be displaced by automation. These changes in the size of the reserve army of the unemployed tend to create downward pressure on wages and exacerbate unemployment, migration and inequality.

The primary sector includes all non-manufacturing workers in the extractive industries like mining, farming and fishing; the secondary sector includes all industrial/manufacturing workers; and the tertiary sector includes service workers in the public and private spheres. The service sector has expanded as more workers have been displaced by automation in farming and manufacturing. Since 1960, the portion of the workforce in manufacturing decreased from 25 percent to about 8.5 percent of the total workforce in the US. About 80 percent of US workers are now employed in the service sector.

At the other end of the workforce spectrum is the mass unemployed, which includes the floating, latent and stagnant unemployed. The floating unemployed is the most mobile and moves more easily (than those displaced in the farming sector) into and out of manufacturing jobs, depending on whether the economy is expanding or contracting. As automation increases, workers in this sector are expected to increase the number of the precarious independent contractors, consultants and freelancers employed in the gig economy. More than 57 million workers in the US are already employed in the gig economy, most of them in temporary, part-time, low-paid jobs, without any job security or benefits.

The latent unemployed, generally less mobile than the floating unemployed, includes workers displaced from the farming sector, who migrate to urban areas where they compete for precarious employment with unemployed manufacturing workers. The stagnant unemployed, the least mobile and fluid sector, includes both those who are able to work and those who cannot work, such as the elderly and the disabled. As deindustrialization of the economy becomes more acute, the floating and latent sectors will increase the ranks of the poor.

In 2016, the United Nations reported an "unprecedented 65 million people displaced by war and persecution in 2015" and over 160 million others living outside their countries of origin. In 1970, there were 9.6 million immigrants in the US, or 4.7 percent of the population; in 2016, there were 43.7 million, or 13.5 percent of the population. Due to economic plight in the less developed world, immigration has continued to shape the US and global workforces.

The rise in global unemployment driven by innovation, which exacerbates economic plight, as well as natural and human-made disasters like wars, all impact migration patterns. As immigrants impact economic, social and cultural dimensions of host countries, what drives the discourse on immigration in host countries are issues of joblessness and the "threat" immigrants pose to their "values" and customs. The solution proposed by many is to demand that governments do more to manage immigration.

A circumspect review of immigration data dispels these myths about immigrants. The truth is that immigrants inject new energy into the economy, academia, arts and sciences, and technological innovation. As political and economic conditions in the US change, however, many immigrants no longer see the US as their first destination. In fact, the 2016 US census reported that citizens who have chosen to live outside the US have more than doubled from 4 million to 9 million between 1999 and 2016.

Toward Radical Change

As attacks on immigrants and labor unions continue, wealth has become more concentrated in the hands of a few billionaire oligarchs. The richest 42 people on the planet control more wealth than the poorest 50 percent of the world's population. In 2017, 57 percent of Americans had less than $1,000 in savings; less than 50 percent of them have less than $400. In 2015, The American Institutes for Research and National Center on Family

Homelessness reported that in the US, there were over 2.5 million homeless in 2012 and between 13.4 million and 16.5 million children living in poverty. Most of Walmart workers earn less than $25,000 last year.

Over the past 40 years, the global economy has followed similar trends. The world's population increased by 3.4 billion and there has been a significant shift toward the service sector, which is also under pressure from automation. The availability of cheap labor as well as high levels of unemployment and the lack of unions in the less industrialized world have maintained and intensified temporary part-time employment that is now trending in many industrialized economies. Twenty percent of organizations globally with more than 1,000 employees have a workforce that is made up of 30 percent or more contingent workers and 162 million people in the US and Europe are engaged in independent work. The US accounts for 53 million. As the gig economy expands, globally, more than 3 billion people live on less than $2.50 per day, and 1.3 billion live on less than $1.25 per day in extreme poverty.

Many retired elderly people employed by Amazon, who gave the best years of their lives to their jobs, now live nomadic lives, in makeshift refugee trailer encampments, which they set up serendipitously in parking lots of big box warehouses where they work. Because many of these people's social security checks are generally less than $1,000 a month, they supplement it by working at Amazon and Walmart warehouses, making sub-standard wages in exchange for robotic 10-hour workdays. They can be fired without notice and don't get paid extra if they take longer than the prescribed time to complete their assigned work. Many of them have said that they work sometimes under horrible workplace conditions without any air conditioning or heating. At the same time they are complimented for their work ethic, they are discouraged from talking to union organizers. It has been reported that Amazon warehouses have set up "Li'l Medics" stations and "Urine Color Charts" outside bathroom walls for workers to check the color of their urine to monitor dehydration and to convey the feeling that the company cares about them.

Sadly, these elderly workers, who are made to compete with younger "gigzombies" in their prime working age, have been known to say that they are happy with what they can get, the opportunity to subject themselves to such humiliation. The working conditions in the gig economy is reminiscent of the horrible working conditions experienced almost a hundred years ago, in the 1930s, by San Francisco longshoremen. There is a well-known example of a reported incident after a 700-pound load accidently dropped on the foot of a longshoreman and broke several bones. Employers placed the worker on the no-hire blacklist because they said he had weak bones.

As economic crises become more frequent and acute, and unemployment, migration and inequality reach unacceptable heights, critics have called for a greater role for government. But these trends are systemic and ubiquitous and, as such, a greater role for government and the gig economy are not solutions to these problems. Mass unemployment is the necessary outcome of the accumulation of wealth. Capitalism is an economy driven by profits, which hampers the development of humanity; when profit investment ventures dry up, the system shuts down. A collectivized system where the fruits of human labor are available to all will set free the forces of labor for the benefit of everyone, not just a few.

Workers—the creators of wealth—want dignified and creative work, with a shorter workweek and a livable wage with benefits, not a gig economy that is automated and stacked with robotic "gigzombies."

In this respect, there are important lessons to learn from the revolutionary tradition in the US. This tradition has a long history that has inspired subsequent generations to demand a world free of misery, impoverishment, exploitation, oppression and class distinctions. They understood that radical change is not just a thing of the past, but that it requires international solidarity, since the alternative is a life of abject poverty.

The Conditions of the Gig Economy Are Unfair and Tumultuous

Nidheesh M. K.

Nidheesh M. K. is a journalist and reporter for Livemint, the digital platform for the Indian daily financial newspaper Mint.

In Kerala, the online economy taps into a labour pool willing to take up transient jobs due to lack of better options. The gig industry is defined as a labour market characterized by the prevalence of short-term contracts or freelance work as opposed to permanent jobs.

The city was fast falling asleep. In home after home, bright porch lights were being turned off behind closed gates. Down an empty street, the light from pole lamps kept flickering over a small gathering of people waiting outside a restaurant. Suddenly, one of their smart phones made a loud factory siren-like sound. It was time to get to work.

As the person reached for a packet of food and drove away on his bike to deliver it to a corner of the city, he waved bye to his co-worker, Sidheek Shahudeen.

Shahudeen does not exactly know how the online food delivery system comes together, but he is hungry for work. He raises his phone to the sky every now and then, hoping for better reception from the cell tower, hoping to land a task faster.

Shahudeen is among thousands of others who found new opportunities in the gig economy and were quick to grab them. But they are fast realizing that this is not exactly what they expected. They are told they are their own bosses, but in reality, little distinguishes them from being a slave to their apps. Their days keep getting longer, the earnings fluctuate and the going gets harder.

"Gig economy has jobs, but long hours, no security and little pay," by Nidheesh M. K., Live Mint, livemint.com, February 8, 2019. Reprinted by permission.

The gig industry is defined as "a labour market characterized by the prevalence of short-term contracts or freelance work as opposed to permanent jobs."

In an increasingly service-oriented job market, the delivery executives for startups such as Uber, Ola, Swiggy and Zomato have been the most visible segment where jobs were created. In fact, NITI Aayog chief executive Amitabh Kant said so in a recent press meet, while countering a leaked government report that stated unemployment in India in 2017-18 touched the highest mark in 45 years. Ola and Uber alone created 2.2 million jobs, Kant said.

Actually, a chunk of these gig economy jobs may not qualify as fresh employment, but what urban affairs expert V. Ravichandar terms "rotating attrition."

"If you look at the profile of people who are getting into Ola, Uber, Swiggy or even startups that offer elder care—these are reasonably educated people in a rotating attrition. People are coming and going from one job to another. People are desperate for jobs, so they take this up and work with some IT company (even if) it is not something they want to do. But they need the income. So they are forced to take that till they can get out of this and do what they want to do," says Ravichandar, also the chairman of Feedback Business Consulting, a business advisory firm.

"They thought life is going to be easy with education. They are finding it's not; therefore, there is a lot of underlying tension and stress that is building up there," he adds.

For Shahudeen, it worked initially. He returned from Dubai some months back, like many fellow Keralites, after he lost his job to increased nationalization there. He then read in the papers that an online food delivery startup was hiring executives 140km away from his village, in Kochi. "I was earning ₹10,000 [$140] per week earlier, now just about ₹800 [$11] per week. But these days, I don't get that many orders. Maybe because a large number of people are joining—each month I think they are adding 500 more men," he says.

But this has not meant a lighter workload. "Most of us work from 12pm to 12am every day. Look at this," he says, pulling up his phone. The screen shows his work log for the last three days of the week. Each day, he clocked between 16-21 hours of work, but his income for three days was below ₹1,000 [$14].

In Kerala, where the unemployment rate is 12.5%, double the national average of 5% according to the 2015 employment survey by India's labour bureau, the online economy taps into a labour pool willing to take up transient jobs due to lack of better opportunities. In other words, they are all searching for a dream job.

"I am happy with this job. This guy (Shahudeen) may have switched on the app and it did not work for him," chips in Ashkar C.A., who joined an online food startup after its competitor terminated his contract for failing to deliver a falooda to a far end of the city without melting, a humanly impossible task. "This company has been really good to me, they even gave ₹35,000 [$490] as medical help during my wife's pregnancy."

Many are yet to come to terms with the fact that they are not employees of the startups they work for. Though they claim to be largely treated well by their employers, all of them agree that they usually labour in difficult conditions. Lack of decent wages, an absence of predefined hours and benefits; the physical strain associated with the work, with all the dust and the heat on the roads; abuse and harassment are among the issues they regularly face. Like many others, they are hit by rising petrol prices. In their case, the rising prices directly eat into their earnings.

This is apart from the usual violence on the streets. Roshin R., who is standing next to Shahudeen, recounts a story. He had an order to deliver to a suburb of the city at night last month, and when he reached the spot he was beaten up by a bunch of goons. They simply did not want to pay for the order. Roshin said he tried to complain to the company, but nobody listened.

Some like Jawahir, a food delivery executive whose ordeal was reported in the local media recently, are trying to channelize the pent-up anger and frustration by unionizing workers.

Some months back, Jawahir arrived at a restaurant to pick up an order and found the owner beating up an employee. He tried to intervene and the owner thrashed him too.

"This whole system depends on how longer and faster you can work, and I am naturally disadvantaged," adds Mukesh V., who is recovering from a stroke that left him unemployed two years ago and could not find a job. His biggest discomfort is the lack of toilets or provision to drink water, something as common as pen and paper for any employee in an office.

Rajesh E., another delivery executive, is struggling to find a balance. He lived a life of comfort until recently, when he moved out of Malaysia. He had lost his job and returned home.

"There is pressure from the family to earn a salary. And I have to repay loans of about ₹20 lakh [$28,000], which I took to migrate to Malaysia. What else to do," he asks, before setting out to deliver an order.

Post midnight, around 1am, one by one, they begin to switch off their apps and leave for home. Like it happens after a factory shift ends, the workforce vanishes within minutes, only to regroup at the same spot the next day.

"All I want to do is to lead an honest life, earn enough so that I don't have to worry about money, bills, food..." Shahudeen says. "I am going to take a week off, I know it will cut short my income. But otherwise, my body will not be able to cope up. I'm not a superman."

The Instability of the Gig Economy Takes a Toll on Workers

Timothy J. Legg

Timothy J. Legg is a professor of nursing at the Rocky Mountain University of Health Professions in Provo, Utah.

W hen Harry Campbell first started working as a rideshare driver in 2014, he was intrigued by the benefits that companies like Uber and Lyft always tout: flexible hours and extra money. But Campbell, who now runs Rideshare Guy, a destination for advice and insight for gig workers, admits that what he found was a lot more than pocket change.

"It's very taxing, both mentally and physically," he explains. "It can be isolating. There's a tendency to always be looking at your phone, always checking the map. The more driving you do, the more stressful it is."

The ability to work whenever you want and earn money at your own rate has been the bedrock of the gig economy, a loosely defined kind of contract work that typically means workers operate as independent contractors, providing services through apps.

These traits also promise to offer relief from the mental health pitfalls of a regular job: no cubicles, no early morning meetings, and no impossible deadlines. Gig workers can pick up shifts around their existing schedules while alleviating some financial strain.

However, where some workers see flexibility, others see a lack of structure that can exacerbate issues like anxiety and depression. The precarious nature of gig economy earnings can increase feelings of stress and added pressure that traditional labor doesn't have. All of which means this promising new free market system can also be extremely damaging for its workers' mental health.

Reprinted from "Here's How the Stress of the Gig Economy Can Affect Your Mental Health" by Timothy J. Legg by permission of Healthline Media, Inc.

Gig Work Offers an Alluring Way to Make Extra Money

With burnout on the rise, more folks are considering the lure of gig economy work. In fact, a 2018 Gallup poll found that around 36 percent of all workers in the United States have some sort of alternative arrangement, whether that's a freelance job, an Etsy shop, or a gig job through an app like TaskRabbit, Instacart, Amazon Fresh, or Uber.

Many people use gig work for extra cash or supplemental income. But for 29 percent of workers, reported Gallup, the alternative arrangement is their primary income.

For Sarah Anne Lloyd, who works as the editor for Curbed Seattle—a stable, unionized, part-time job—gig work has helped round out her income.

"For the past two years, I've had a part-time job and have relied more heavily on gigs. Some of those are freelance writing—more my chosen career—but I also contract with a cat-sitting company," she says. She also spent some time as a Postmates driver and notes that she recently finished her certification as a yoga instructor, which she describes as "gig work more often than not."

For People with Mental Health Conditions, Gig Work Offers an Alternative Approach to the Workforce

For those living with certain mental health conditions, gig work also offers an alternative entrance into the workforce. Surveys of national data indicate that these individuals face higher rates of unemployment and tend to earn much less per year.

But working is also a critical component of mental health, says Dr. Yavar Moghimi, chief psychiatric medical officer for AmeriHealth Caritas.

"It's a big, big way that people find meaning in their life. It keeps them interacting with people on a regular basis. It's a major social outlet, talking to co-workers or having that conversation with customers."

Moghimi says that for many individuals living with mental health issues, the normal job search process can be difficult. The gig economy can, instead, offer another avenue, especially if it avoids the traditional pitfalls of an unhealthy work environment, like poor communication and management practices or unclear tasks and organizational objectives.

In theory, the gig economy could avoid these strains, as app-based gigs make it clear where workers are supposed to be and when. In practice, though, the structures of gig work—like a lack of managerial support or community and punitive rating systems—present numerous additional risk factors.

Unrealistic Expectations and Money Uncertainties Cause Huge Mental Strain

One of the most damaging aspects of the gig economy is the feeling that workers can never really earn as much as they're promised. Numerous reports have found that most Uber and Lyft drivers earn less than promised. One report from Earnest found that 45 percent of Uber drivers earn less than $100 per month. This is, in large part, due to unrealistic expectations of gig workers, which can lead to huge mental strain.

Lloyd found this to be true when she was driving for Postmates, a food delivery service.

"One time I was driving for Postmates in North Seattle, and I got an assignment to deliver from a Taco Time just barely within my call range to someone just barely inside a lower payment tier. The whole ordeal took me almost an hour—between getting to the Taco Time, waiting for the order to be ready, and getting to the front door—and the client didn't tip, so I made $4 from the whole ordeal," she explains.

"Basically, I made $4 an hour, less than a third of Seattle's minimum wage."

Poverty is, on its own, a mental illness risk factor. Stress over money and debt can lead to increased anxiety symptoms and even exacerbate symptoms of PTSD. Living in a constant high level of stress creates a flood of hormones like cortisol, which can lead to physical reactions, including high blood pressure and digestive inflammation.

"When you're operating under that [poverty] mindset, it becomes very hard to prioritize other needs," Moghimi says. "Everything else kind of gets dropped for the pursuit of whatever the next bar is."

It can also make it next to impossible to take care of your mental health. Because for all of the talk about flexibility, working in an on-demand industry like food delivery or ridesharing means that some shifts—usually the hardest, most hectic ones—are just worth more.

"Drivers have to plan shifts around the times and places with the most demand to actually make the kind of money that's estimated in those recruiting ads," Lloyd says, who saw it in her own work and as someone who uses apps. "More than once I've gotten a Lyft driver that lives an hour or two away from the city and braves the long commute in the early morning to make more money, or has to drive back in the wee hours."

Campbell, too, says that the fear of not earning enough, or not maximizing your earning hours, is what keeps drivers chained to their phone. He says drivers that "chase the surge" will often be "picking up their phones all night" to see if there's even a little bit more money to be made. If they don't, it could be the difference between putting gas in the car for the next shift or making rent. The stakes, in that way, are high. And that can be physically, mentally, and emotionally draining.

Moghimi says that when gig work is purely supplemental—on top of disability pay or in addition to a spouse's income, for example—it can be positive. But for those who are relying on their gig work full time to pay the bills, it can exacerbate existing issues. Campbell agrees, stating that even though he's made a career out of driving for rideshare companies, it's "not a sustainable, long-term" job.

Gig Workers Take On Similar Challenges as Small Business Owners, but Without Many of the Benefits

Gig workers are, as Lyft and Uber will tell you, small business owners. They take on many of the same challenges, like figuring out complicated taxes and insurance issues and paying the federal self-employment tax, which adds up to a total of 15.3 percent.

They have to calculate their mileage and be diligent with their spending. They may even have to pay local business taxes, which can cancel out any additional earnings.

Unfortunately, they often miss out on the built-in benefits of regular jobs *and* other flexible work, like freelancing independently or working remotely.

"Being able to work from home has vastly improved my mental health," Lloyd says. "But it's the freelance work, not the more traditional gig work, that lets me stay at home." The gig work, she explains, is what keeps her chained to an app, driving across town, hoping for good ratings.

Unlike other flexible work, gig work relies on customer service and pleasing the user. Both Uber and Lyft require drivers to maintain a rating of 4.6 stars, says Campbell. This means most riders have to give a perfect score, and drivers can be deactivated if riders don't rate them highly enough.

"You're doing everything you can to keep your rating, but you're seeing other drivers getting deactivated left and right for things they can't control," says Chris Palmer, who delivered for DoorDash, another food delivery system. As an example, he says, "If the food isn't prepared right, we get a bad rating."

While Some Companies Offer Healthcare Options, It's Often Still Unaffordable

One of the longest-standing benefits of traditional work has been access to healthcare. To catch up, apps like Uber and Lyft have worked to make it accessible. Uber has partnered with Stride, a platform that helps people find an insurance provider. But those healthcare plans are often still not affordable; without employee subsidies, healthcare costs continue to skyrocket for gig workers.

"I pay for my own healthcare, and one of the reasons I gig and freelance is because I need to pay for my care," says Lloyd, who sees a therapist and uses medication. "Since I started buying an exchange plan [healthcare offered through the state] two years ago, my premium has gone up more than $170 *per month*."

Access to affordable insurance is one barrier to receiving mental healthcare, but it's certainly not the only one. Many Americans who live with mental illness are insured but still unable to get into a functional treatment program. In fact, while an estimated 5.3 million Americans live with acute mental illness and have no insurance at all, nearly five times that number are insured but aren't in treatment.

There are a variety of reasons why an insured person might not be in treatment. Shortages of professionals, including therapists and counselors, put mental healthcare out of reach for folks with unpredictable schedules and no paid time off.

People often have to make several contacts with psychiatric offices and can expect to wait, on average, just under a month to get in for their first appointment. Once they're in, those appointments might feel rushed, and there's no way to meet with several providers to find the best fit.

The American Psychological Association advises that the optimal number of treatments is up to 30 appointments in a six-month span, or weekly appointments for 12 to 16 weeks. As many as 20 percent of patients, they say, drop out prematurely. Other research has found 50 percent drop out by the third session.

Transitioning Into More Traditional Work Has Been a Game Changer for Some

Typical job benefits, like sick days, subsidized healthcare, and reliable income can all be massively beneficial to those who are living with mental illness. Palmer, who says he was "not well" while he was delivering for DoorDash, says that transitioning into a more traditional job has been a game changer.

"Stability has been key," he explains.

That describes perhaps the biggest challenge the gig economy poses to the mental health of its workers. Though companies promise flexibility, there are added stressors that go along with gig work, which can be compounded by the ways that contract work fails to support the people who do it.

"The gig economy takes advantage of laws designed for freelancing and small business-building," Lloyd says. "They treat working for yourself like working for somebody else."

That disconnect results in unpredictable wages, particularly as more and more alternatives flood the market. Companies like Instacart have used the contractor model to avoid paying federal or state minimum wages, using customer tips as part of the wage algorithm. This meant that when a customer "tipped" their delivery person, they were actually just paying them for their service while the app took a cut.

When labor activists with Working Washington, who Palmer now volunteers with, complained about the practice, Instacart changed its payment structure twice in a matter of weeks.

When the wages are unsteady and highly motivated by the whims of customers, there's a precarious balance. The daily stress of managing expenses like gas, mileage, and customer service, as well as the added difficulty of affording and finding mental healthcare, can leave some gig workers feeling more fried than they would in a 9-to-5.

That said, the contract model can be a massive relief for some workers, especially those who have lived with a long-term mental illness. The ability to set their own hours, coupled with part-time work that might enable them to also receive disability or other assistance, is unique in a labor market that's traditionally been unwelcoming for folks needing accommodations.

If the companies that make up the behemoth gig economy can continue to listen to workers and meet their needs—whether it's grace around star ratings, assistance with healthcare costs, or ensuring a living base wage—it may continue to add value. Without some serious safety nets, though, the gig economy will continue to be a solution for some but a potential mental health risk for many.

CHAPTER 2

Does the Gig Economy Fill a Need in the Labor Market?

The Relationship Between Workers and Employers in the Gig Economy Is Complicated

Jeffery Marino

Jeffery Marino is a journalist and reporter for ZipRecruiter, an American employment marketplace for job seekers and employers.

We still aren't exactly sure how many people are working in the gig economy. But lots of people are trying to figure it out. The Bureau of Labor Statistics (BLS) recently released its highly anticipated study on "alternative employment arrangements" and reported that freelancers comprised 10.1% of the workforce as of May 2017. This figure represents, unbelievably, about a 1% decline from the last time the survey was conducted in 2005.

Given the initial BLS study predates the invention of the iPhone in 2007, and was conducted well before gig economy-goliath Uber was founded in 2009, we're dubious of these results, to say the least. Thankfully, we have access to real-time data of our own from the millions of employers and job seekers who use ZipRecruiter every day.

We marshaled these resources to develop a comprehensive study of both the people working in the gig economy and the companies who want to hire them. First, we launched a ZipRecruiter survey in April of this year and connected with over 9,000 active job seekers (a robust and representative sample) to take their temperature on the gig economy.

Then, ZipRecruiter's Senior Labor Economist Mitch Downey dug into about 5 million job openings in our database and determined what drives firms to hire contract workers and where the paths of each group converge or collide.

Overall, we uncovered several frictions pointing to a mismatch between workers in the gig economy and the employers who want

"Rethinking The Relationship Between Gig Economy Workers And Employers," by Jeffery Marino, ZipRecruiter. Reprinted by permission.

to hire them. We also gained some insight into how to bring them closer together.

An Anatomy of the Gig Worker

There are lots of free agents on the job market, and most of them are in between gigs. Of the 9,000 job seekers we surveyed, 25% identified as a worker in the gig economy (far more than BLS estimates). However, when asked how many gigs they currently have, the majority of respondents (38%) said they are between gigs. An additional 35% indicated they currently only have one gig, which could mean they are working in a full-time contract position, or that they are looking for additional work.

Either way, it's clear from our survey that the vast majority of those working in the gig economy are looking for more opportunities. When asked if they'd prefer to replace their current contract job with full-time employment, 81% said they would like to work one, full-time job. A mere 5% responded they already have a full-time job.

A synthesis of these results challenges the idea that workers are using the opportunities offered by the gig economy as a side hustle. Rather, they are approaching what is essentially part-time work as a full-time job. This becomes even more apparent when you consider that 65% of respondents said their gig economy job was their sole source of income.

More than 27% of our survey-takers reported they're working in the gig economy because they are in between permanent jobs. But this doesn't mean people are approaching this type of work as a last resort. Twelve percent said it is because it works great with their schedule and 10% said it allows them to pursue their passion.

The majority, however, chose "all of the above," a result revealing mixed feelings over the tradeoffs that come with this work. Based on the narrative responses to these questions, the number one tradeoff is clear: independent contractors love the flexibility and hate the instability that comes with gig work.

Many of the freelancers we surveyed said they chose their path out of frustration with traditional employment. Two key sticking points for a number of respondents were the length of time the hiring process takes and the lack of a flexible work schedule. When asked how they feel about the gig economy, the words "freedom" and "flexibility" appeared in more than 200 of the 1,400 written responses we received.

When asked about their highest level of education, 32%—the largest segment of respondents—said they hold a graduate degree, and 31% have a 4-year degree. This could indicate that many freelancers are overqualified for the full-time positions available today, but it also reveals the large share of highly- educated workers currently untapped by traditional employers.

Companies with the Greatest Demand for Contractors

Several characteristics stood out among organizations who post the greatest share of contract positions. They tend to be large companies with 100 or more employees, and operate in rapidly changing industries that require specialized skills and college degrees.

We compared millions of job postings for contract positions by company size and found that larger organizations hire more contractors. Broadly speaking, these companies can be split into two groups: Those with 50 or fewer employees (where 5-7% of openings are for contractors) and those with 500 or more employees (where 10-15% of openings are contract posts).

Industries with occupations where the demand for different types of skills is constantly in flux also tend to hire more contractors. To determine which industries experience more change in the skills they need from their employees, we first looked at the occupations within every industry and then calculated how these sets of occupations changed between 2012 and 2017. The industries that showed the most occupational change over time were engineering and science, energy and environment, and tourism and travel.

Jobs posted to ZipRecruiter within these industries had a greater share of available contract positions when compared to the other industries, which had little to no change.

Educational attainment also stood out as a determining factor for the employee vs. contractor choice. We looked at every occupation designated by the Census Bureau and calculated the fraction of posts that specifically list a Bachelor's degree as one of the qualifications. Then we compared rates of contractor openings and rates of Bachelor's degree requirements across those occupations.

We discovered that jobs requiring a college degree are more likely to be filled by contractors. The occupations that rarely require a college degree are roughly half as likely to look for contractors as those which most frequently require one.

The Mismatch and Proposed Solutions

Once you hold these two respective profiles side-by-side, it's clear that contractors have what companies want: They're well-educated, flexible, and available to work. The mismatch arises when these companies don't offer them what they desire most: stability.

We know that large companies pay more and offer the best benefits. Unfortunately, these same benefits are not extended to independent contractors. This cost savings is precisely why larger companies are more likely to post contract positions.

This begs the question: is this all-or-nothing approach necessary? Offering a modicum of benefits, such as access to flexible spending accounts or company-subsidized training may entice the vast majority of contractors looking for traditional employment off the sidelines. Gig economy employers who best address the desire for stability among the workforce will undoubtedly win out.

Flexibility is one confluence we found on both sides of our study. Employers operating in fast-changing industries need nimble talent and gig economy-workers enjoy having a say over where and when they work. Traditional employers have answered this call by being more liberal with work-from-home policies and offering things like unlimited paid time off. But this doesn't typically apply to independent contractors.

Firms with constantly changing needs favor contractors because they can replace them at will. But some consideration for a stable and flexible work schedule could still apply during the terms of the contract. Just because an employer hasn't made the commitment to full-time employment doesn't mean they shouldn't offer paid time off to someone who's working a six-month project. After all, most employment is at-will anyways.

The basic equation is simple: contract employees enjoy the benefits of not being tethered to a 9-to-5, but the lack of support and stability offered by their contract employers greatly outweighs this benefit. Our survey shows there's a large talent pool in the gig economy in search of full-time employment. Firms in need of that talent may do well to take a closer look at the stability they offer their full-time employees and consider sharing some of that wealth with the workers they wish to hire on contract.

The Gig Economy Offers Numerous Benefits to Workers and Consumers

Séamus Nevin

Séamus Nevin is the chief economist of the UK's Education Endowment Fund.

The world of work is being transformed, driven by rapid developments in technology, globalisation, and demographic change. Now, the concept of "employment" itself seems to be increasingly past its sell-by date. A proliferation of new, online platforms has made access to paid work easier and more efficient than ever before by instantaneously connecting people who have work they need to be done with others willing to do the task.

The "gig" economy has made it easy for workers to control when, where and how much they choose to work. In addition, the flexible nature of gig work offers benefits to employers, as they only pay when work is done, and don't incur staff costs when customer demand is not there. These disruptive changes offer the potential to boost growth and deliver more opportunities for both workers and consumers. However, they also have the potential to increase insecurity at work for some.

Figures from the Labour Force Survey (LFS) and the ONS suggest that easier routes into self-employment have led to rising participation in the labour force for those who have historically struggled to get into work; notably single parents, disabled individuals, and the long-term unemployed. Over half the part-time self-employed workforce is female and the number of women in self-employment has grown at around twice the rate as men over recent years.

Older people, too, are increasingly choosing self-employment. Around one in three of those who work in their late 60s are going

"Gig economy: Disruption can bring benefits for workers and consumers," by Séamus Nevin, London School of Economics, June 8, 2017. Reprinted by permission.

it alone, a figure that rises to almost half for the growing number of people working past the age of 70. Self-employment is also becoming a more important source of work for young people, the number of under-25s going into conventional employment instead of self-employment has actually fallen since 2000. Political parties of all persuasions have supported this trend.

We should also be wary of the narrative that these jobs are predominantly of the low-wage, low-quality caricature; a picture often painted by their detractors. According to the Resolution Foundation, a left-leaning think tank, the gig jobs that have seen the highest rate of growth over the last decade are in typically high wage sectors, including a 90 per cent increase in public administration positions, a 60 per cent increase in banking jobs, and a 100 per cent increase in advertising roles. Meanwhile, growth of self-employment in the taxi profession—one of the most widely scrutinised types of gig work—has been a relatively low 7 per cent.

Nevertheless, of the nearly 3 million people who have found a new job since 2008, around 45 per cent have been classed as self-employed such that one in seven workers in the UK is now working for his/her-self. Consequently, HM Revenue and Customs are becoming increasingly concerned about the growing impact on the public finances, because self-employment is taxed at a lower rate than traditional employment. The Office for Budget Responsibility (OBR) has estimated that, on current trends, by 2020-21 the increase in self-employment will have cost the Treasury £3.5 billion. At a time of ongoing national belt-tightening, this growing hole in the tax take is becoming increasingly hard for politicians to ignore.

The rise of self-employment, together with the public profile of new companies in the gig economy, has focused debate about whether employment regulations and practices are keeping pace with the changing world of work. While relatively new gig economy firms have been the focus of much recent public and media attention, gig type work itself is nothing new. Internet-based platforms have simply altered the manner in which some people source gig work. Indeed, the majority of the increase in self-employment since 2008 has actually been in historically conventional types of work including administrative and support service activities; information and communication; and health and social work. As such, the challenges thrown up at the boundary between self-employment and employment are not new.

While much of the focus has been on the use of online technologies, the trend towards increased levels of self-employment is what really matters. Viewed in this context, new platforms and innovative new business practices have the ability to expand routes into work and provide a lifeline to those that find themselves displaced in a shifting economic environment.

Nevertheless, the rise of the "gig economy" has raised questions about what it really means to be self-employed. One problem is that the theoretically binary divide between employment and self-employment understates the level of complexity that exists in practice. There is little clarity in statutory definitions of employment status, although there is a body of case law. For the purposes of employment rights, an individual's employment status is categorised as one of three types—employee, worker, or self-employed—while for tax purposes, that individual can be categorised as one of two types—either employee or self-employed. In some circumstances, because employment law and tax law follow different statutes, it is even possible for an individual to be categorised as an employee for the purposes of employment rights, and self-employed for tax purposes.

This arbitrage highlights the other challenge that arises from the murky divide between the established definitions of employment and self-employment: individuals, who may have many of the characteristics of being employed, nevertheless lack the rights and protections of employed workers. We must recognise that self-employment is not without its perils and pitfalls. Statutory sick pay, statutory maternity pay, training support and employer pension contributions are some of the occupational benefits individuals forgo when they become technically self-employed. The self-employment landscape in the UK is in clear need of simplification and clarity.

Evidence suggests that a lack of clarity and certainty is resulting in confusion for both businesses and workers. The Government's own Dean Review found evidence that a lack of clarity is resulting in confusion for both businesses and workers. Indeed, data from HMRC suggests that more than 5.5 million people report income from self-employment; but that almost 1.8 million of those people also report income from employment. In other words, approximately one-third of people who believe themselves to be self-employed are actually, or also, in contracted employment. A consequence is that, in certain circumstances, firms can be reluctant to do more to help self-employed individuals understand their rights and entitlements because doing so risks their relationship appearing like an employer-employee relationship should they be subject to an employment status challenge in court.

There is a strong case for improving people's understanding of their employment status, as well as the rights, responsibilities and trade-offs that come with working in different types of employment. Improving the rights and protections of vulnerable workers in a sustainable way without damaging the availability of work opportunities or economic growth is a difficult but important objective.

For Some, the Gig Economy Offers a Key Way to Make Ends Meet

Elka Torpey and Andrew Hogan

Elka Torpey and Andrew Hogan are economists with the US Bureau of Labor Statistics.

R yan Heenan works whenever, wherever. He's a songwriter who sells customized jingles and videos online to clients worldwide. "It's really a dream come true," says Heenan. "It gives me the freedom to set my own hours. And I can do what I do anywhere there's an Internet connection."

Heenan is one of many people in the so-called gig economy. But there is no official definition of the "gig economy"—or, for that matter, a gig. For purposes of this article, a gig describes a single project or task for which a worker is hired, often through a digital marketplace, to work on demand.

Some gigs are a type of short-term job, and some workers pursue gigs as a self-employment option; those concepts aren't new. However, companies connecting workers with these jobs through websites or mobile applications (more commonly known as apps) is a more recent development.

Keep reading to learn what gigs are all about and how some workers are taking a gig approach to earning money. You'll gain insight into the pros and cons of gig work, along with suggestions for getting started.

The Gig Workforce

Gig workers are spread among diverse occupation groups and are not easily identified in surveys of employment and earnings. But they are similar in the way they earn money.

"Working in a gig economy," by Elka Torpey and Andrew Hogan, Bureau of Labor Statistics, May 2016. Reprinted by permission.

These workers often get individual gigs using a website or mobile app that helps to match them with customers. Some gigs may be very brief, such as answering a 5-minute survey. Others are much longer but still of limited duration, such as an 18-month database management project. When one gig is over, workers who earn a steady income this way must find another. And sometimes, that means juggling multiple jobs at once.

For example, TyKecia Hayes is a freelance filmmaker in Los Angeles, California. When she's between filmmaking projects, Hayes picks up gigs that include working as a personal assistant, helping people move, and making deliveries. "I'm able to work when I need money and take off when I need to," she says. "That's the beauty of it."

Counting Gig Workers

You may have heard a lot of buzz about growth in the gig economy. But government data sources have difficulty counting how many gig workers there are. Among the sources that may shed light on this topic are data from the US Bureau of Labor Statistics (BLS) and the US Census Bureau.

BLS Data

Gig workers could be in contingent or alternative employment arrangements, or both, as measured by BLS. Contingent workers are those who don't have an implicit or explicit contract for long-term employment. Alternative employment arrangements include independent contractors (also called freelancers or independent consultants), on-call workers, and workers provided by temporary help agencies or contract firms.

The data BLS has for these types of workers are about a decade old. In 2005, contingent workers accounted for roughly 2 to 4 percent of all workers. About 7 percent of workers were independent contractors, the most common alternative employment arrangement, in that year. BLS plans to collect these data again in May 2017.

Other, more recent, data from BLS likely reflect a lot of gig work, but these workers are not broken out separately. For example, gig workers may be included in counts of workers who are part-time, self-employed, or hold multiple jobs. But these counts also include workers who are not part of the gig workforce.

Census Data

Nonemployer statistics data, created by the Census Bureau from tax data provided by the Internal Revenue Service (IRS), offer another possible look at what's been happening in the gig economy. Many gig workers fit the Census definition of a nonemployer: in most cases, a self-employed individual operating a very small, unincorporated business with no paid employees.

Between 2003 and 2013, all industry sectors experienced growth in nonemployer businesses. The "other services" sector gained nearly 1 million nonemployer businesses during that time, the most of any sector. Many of the occupations in this sector involve on-demand services, such as petsitting and appliance repair, making them well suited to gig employment.

Occupations for Gig Employment

Gigs are more likely in some occupations than in others. Work that involves a single task, such as writing a business plan, lends itself well to this type of arrangement. Any occupation in which workers may be hired for on-demand jobs has the potential for gig employment.

The BLS Occupational Outlook Handbook (*OOH*) covers about 83 percent of the jobs in the US economy. Its 329 detailed profiles of occupations are sorted by group. This section highlights some of those groups in which gig work may be increasingly relevant, giving examples of occupations in each.

Arts and Design

Many occupations in this group, including musicians, graphic designers, and craft and fine artists, offer specific one-time services or customized products, which makes them good candidates for gig work.

Computer and Information Technology

Web developers, software developers, and computer programmers are among the occupations in this group in which workers might be hired to complete a single job, such as to create a small-business website or a new type of software.

Construction and Extraction

Carpenters, painters, and other construction workers frequently take on individual projects of short duration, a hallmark of gig jobs.

Media and Communications

The services of technical writers, interpreters and translators, photographers, and others in this group are often project-based and easy to deliver electronically, fueling a market for gig workers.

Transportation and Material Moving

Ridesharing apps have helped to create opportunities for workers who provide transportation to passengers as needed, and on-demand shopping services have led to gig jobs for delivery drivers.

Pros and Cons of Gig Work

Gig workers may do varied tasks, but they have similar things they enjoy—and don't—about their arrangements.

Freedom to work as they please is what many people like, but with autonomy comes responsibility. For example, it can be stressful for gig workers to ensure that they have consistent income. "When you're a freelancer, you make the decisions, which is fantastic," says Theresa Anderson of Las Vegas, Nevada, who does graphic design projects part time from her home. "But it can also be really scary."

Pros

Gig workers say that they like being in control. They can choose projects they enjoy and schedule their work around their lives.

Flexibility

People who want to work without having set hours may look for gigs to fit their schedules. "I log on and work when I want," says Ariana Baseman, a rideshare driver in Detroit, Michigan, who transports passengers in her spare time, in addition to working a traditional, full-time job. "It's that flexible."

Like other types of flexible employment arrangements, gigs may offer workers an option for adaptability. "The thing that I love about it is the freedom," says Nick Walter, of Salt Lake City, Utah, who creates online classes in computer programming. "If you decide you want to go on vacation, you can do that."

Variety

Gigs may provide workers with a chance to try several types of jobs. As a result, they present variety and career exploration to both new and experienced workers. "Take opportunities when they arise," says Heenan. "You have a lot of chances to do different things."

And if you're a "people person," gig work may offer interaction with a diverse clientele. "I love that I get to constantly work with different people," says Hayes. "I'm pretty social, so I enjoy meeting all types."

Passion

You might want to select gigs the same way you would traditional employment: by finding work in which you pursue your interests. And depending on how you schedule your gigs, you might be able to choose among many passions.

Some workers take gigs that allow them to encourage others in a field they enjoy. For example, retired business owner Tamma Ford of Seattle, Washington, takes consulting gigs that let her share her expertise with people who are just getting started.

Cons

There's a lot of uncertainty associated with gig work. For example, you'll need to have a steady stream of gigs to get consistent pay. Even then, the amount you earn may not offset some of the costs you'll be responsible for outside of a traditional employment relationship, such as benefits.

Inconsistency

Landing enough work to provide a stable income from gigs alone isn't always easy, or even possible. As a result, many gig workers find gigs adequate for part-time work but not a full-time career.

Workers may struggle with looking for jobs, not knowing what—if anything—will come next. "Sometimes you're not making any money because you're not getting any work," says Baseman. "That part's not really in your control." And even after you complete a gig, you may face periods of no income if there are delays in getting paid.

Scheduling

Not having set hours or an employer who provides direction for the day is challenging for some gig workers. "Unless you're a very dedicated, self-motivated individual, it can be hard to focus," says Walter. "There's no one telling you what to do, no deadlines."

And depending on the gig, you may need to work nonstandard days or times to finish a job. If you get a gig requiring hours on the weekend, for example, you might not be able to spend time with friends who have traditional 9-to-5 workweeks.

Lack of Benefits

Gig workers don't usually get employer-paid benefits, such as premiums on health insurance and contributions to retirement plans. You'll need to research these topics and pay for the products yourself. "I took things like health insurance for granted," says Heenan of his former job, working at a school. "When you freelance, you have to find those things on your own, and it's expensive."

Other benefits that gig workers often miss out on are annual leave and sick leave. Like any employees who don't get paid time off, no work means no pay.

Getting Gigs

There are different ways to get started in the gig economy. Identify what you do well and what you might enjoy doing. Then, search for opportunities while keeping in mind some practical matters.

Create Your Niche

Think about the types of services you might be able to offer. What skills, experience, or other assets do you have that you can share? Consider that some gigs are for general tasks and others require a specific skillset.

Learn from Others

When you have an idea of the type of work you'd like to do, talk to people who are already doing it. Or browse blogs or other resources to learn from the experiences of others.

Scoping out the market for your services will help you determine how much to charge—or even whether you should pursue your plan. "Start to get a feel for the value of your work," says Orlando Rivera, who does general handiwork and construction, among other tasks, in Brooklyn, New York. Ford learned a lot by looking at the profiles of others who were doing the types of tasks she wanted to do: nonfiction writing, translation, and business consulting.

Stand Out

Figure out ways to differentiate yourself from other workers, such as by offering a service that is unique or in high demand. You might want to consider becoming self-employed as a way to fill that niche.

As mentioned previously, gig workers may be counted among workers who are self-employed. Some industries are projected to have more growth than others in the number of self-employed jobs over the 2014–24 decade. For example, home health care services is projected to grow rapidly and add many self-employed jobs over the decade.

Find Opportunities

Many gig workers use a platform (usually a third-party company that has a website or an app) to help connect them with jobs. But others find work off platform (such as through networking). Still others get gigs from both sources.

Sign Up

Applying to work with a gig platform may involve providing information about yourself and your services. If you create a profile, be sure it's professional and complete.

But, Walter cautions, consider taking gigs on the side until you're sure you like working this way. "All these places make it so easy to just jump in and start doing something," he says. "Get signed up and try it. But don't quit your day job."

Consider Off-Platform Work

With some types of work, you may be able to find jobs without the help of an intermediary. Many gig platforms take a cut of the money paid for services, so your work may be more profitable if you find jobs yourself.

To get gigs off platform, you might advertise your services by distributing flyers or posting on a website. You might also try to drum up business by connecting through community associations or your local chamber of commerce.

Build Your Base

Regardless of how you get gigs, referrals and positive feedback from clients are key. If you build a reputation for quality work, people may be more likely to seek you out for future gigs.

In fact, successful gig workers often say that many of their jobs are from repeat business. "Treat every task as an opportunity to perform your best," says Rivera, "and have fun while you're at it."

Be Realistic

Deciding to take a gig approach to earning money requires patience, budgeting, and adaptability.

Give It Time

Expect that it will take time to learn what works, and what doesn't, when pursuing gigs. It may take a few tries before you figure out which keywords to use when searching for jobs, for example. And even then, it could take months to get gigs regularly.

Anderson started out doing graphic design gigs as a hobby for about a year, eventually building up to 10 to 15 hours per week of supplemental income. "Don't think you're going to make a fortune overnight," she says.

Manage Money

Even if you're patient about making money, you should have a backup plan: figure out what you'll do for income if you don't get enough gig work to pay the bills. You might want to work a more traditional job, in addition to doing gigs, at least at first.

Managing finances is an important part of making gig arrangements viable. As a gig worker, you'll need to keep track of the money you earn. You should also set aside some of your income for other purposes, such as an emergency fund for unplanned expenses.

Be Adaptable

Not every gig is a good fit, and it's okay to trust your instincts. "If it doesn't feel right," says Ford, "let it go." Gig workers also advise changing tactics when what you're doing isn't going well.

To stay competitive in the gig economy, be prepared to keep learning. For example, Anderson takes advantage of free graphic design tutorials whenever they're offered, keeping her skills current to grow her business over time. "The more I do graphic design, the more I love it," she says of her gig work. "I genuinely want to do this and make it a career."

Millennials Are Less Interested in Traditional Work

Bernhard Resch

Bernhard Resch is a researcher in organizational politics at the University of St. Gallen in Switzerland. His research focuses on self-organized work practices.

Uber suffered a legal blow this week when a California judge granted class action status to a lawsuit claiming the car-hailing service treats its drivers like employees, without providing the necessary benefits.

Up to 160,000 Uber chauffeurs are now eligible to join the case of three drivers demanding the company pay for health insurance and expenses such as mileage. Some say a ruling against the company could doom the business model of the on-demand or "sharing" economy that Uber, Upwork and TaskRabbit represent.

Whatever the outcome, it's unlikely to reverse the most radical reinvention of work since the rise of industrialization—a massive shift toward self-employment typified by on-demand service apps and enabled by technology. That's because it's not a trend driven solely by these tech companies.

Workers themselves, especially millennials, are increasingly unwilling to accept traditional roles as cogs in the corporate machinery being told what to do. Today, 34% of the US workforce freelances, a figure that is estimated to reach 50% by 2020. That's up from the 31% estimated by the Government Accountability Office in a 2006 study.

"Labor 2.0: why we shouldn't fear the 'sharing economy' and the reinvention of work," by Bernhard Resch, The Conversation, September 4, 2015, https://theconversation. com/labor-2-0-why-we-shouldnt-fear-the-sharing-economy-and-the-reinvention-of-work-46959. Licensed under CC BY-ND 4.0 International.

Rise of the Gig-Based Economy

In place of the traditional notion of long-term employment and the benefits that came with it, app-based platforms have given birth to the gig-based economy, in which workers create a living through a patchwork of contract jobs.

Uber and Lyft connect drivers to riders. TaskRabbit helps someone who wants to remodel a kitchen or fix a broken pipe find a nearby worker with the right skills. Airbnb turns everyone into hotel proprietors, offering their rooms and flats to strangers from anywhere.

Thus far, the industries where this transformation has occurred have been fairly low-skilled, but that's changing. Start-ups Medicast, Axiom and Eden McCallum are now targeting doctors, legal workers and consultants for short-term contract-based work.

A 2013 study estimated that almost half of US jobs are at risk of being replaced by a computer within 15 years, signaling most of us may not have a choice but to accept a more tenuous future.

The economic term referring to this transformation of how goods and services are produced is "platform capitalism," in which an app and the engineering behind it bring together customers in neat novel economic ecosystems, cutting out traditional companies.

But is the rise of the gig economy a bad thing, as Democratic front-runner Hillary Clinton suggested in July when she promised to "crack down on bosses misclassifying workers as contractors"?

While some contend this sweeping change augurs a future of job insecurity, impermanence and inequality, others see it as the culmination of a utopia in which machines will do most of the labor and our workweeks will be short, giving us all more time for leisure and creativity.

My recent research into self-organized work practices suggests the truth lies somewhere in between. Traditional hierarchies provide a certain security, but they also curb creativity. A new economy in which we are increasingly masters of our jobs as well as our lives provides opportunities to work for things that matter to us and invent new forms of collaboration with fluid hierarchies.

Sharing into the Abyss?

Critics such as essayist Evgeny Morozov or the philosopher Byung-Chul Han highlight the dark side of this "sharing economy."

Instead of a collaborative commons, they envision the commercialization of intimate life. In this view, the likes of Uber and Airbnb are perverting the initial collaborative nature of their business models—car-sharing and couch-surfing—adding a price and transforming them from shared goods into commercial products. The unspoken assumption is that you have the choice between renting and owning, but "renting" will be the default option for the majority.

Idealists take another tack. Part of the on-demand promise is that technology makes it easier to share not only cultural products but also cars, houses, tools or even renewable energy. Add increasing automation to the picture and it invokes a society in which work is no longer the focus. Instead, people spend more of their time in creative and leisurely activities. Less drudge, more time to think.

The "New Work movement," formed by philosopher Frithjof Bergmann in the late 1980s, envisioned such a future, while economist and social theorist Jeremy Rifkin imagines consumers and producers becoming one and the same: prosumers.

From Self-Employment to Self-Organization

Both of these extremes seem to miss the mark. In my view, the most decisive development underlying this discussion is the need for worker self-organization as the artificial wall between work and life dissolves.

My recent work has involved studying how the relationship between managers and workers has evolved, from traditional structures that are top-down, with employees doing what they're told, to newer ones that boast self-managing teams with managers counseling them or even the complete abolition of formal hierarchies of rank.

While hierarchy guarantees a certain security and offers a lot of stability, its absence frees us to work more creatively and collaboratively. When we're our own boss we bear more responsibility, but also more reward.

And as we increasingly self-organize alongside others, people start to experiment in various ways, from peer to peer and open source projects to social entrepreneurship initiatives, bartering circles and new forms of lending.

The toughest tension for workers will be how best to balance private and work-related demands as they are increasingly interwoven.

Avoiding the Pitfalls of Platform Capitalism

Another risk is that we will become walled in by the platform capitalism being built by Uber and TaskRabbit but also Google, Amazon and Apple, in which companies control their respective ecosystems. Thus, our livelihoods remain dependent on them, like in the old model, just without the benefits workers have fought for many decades.

In his recent book "Postcapitalism," Paul Mason eloquently puts it like this: "the main contradiction today is between the possibility of free, abundant goods and information; and a system of monopolies, banks and governments trying to keep things private, scarce and commercial."

To avoid this fate, it's essential to create sharing and on-demand platforms that follow a non-market rationale, such as through open source technologies and nonprofit foundations, to avoid profit overriding all other considerations. The development of the operating system Linux and web browser Firefox are examples of the possibility and merits of these models.

Between Hell and Heaven

Millennials grew up in the midst of the birth of a new human age, with all the world's knowledge at their fingertips. As they take over the workforce, the traditional hierarchies that have long dictated work will continue to crumble.

Socialized into the participatory world of the web, millennials prefer to self-organize in a networked way using readily available communication technology, without bosses dictating goals and deadlines.

But this doesn't mean we'll all be contractors. Frederic Laloux and Gary Hamel have shown in their impressive research that a surprisingly broad range of companies have already acknowledged these realities. Amazon-owned online shoe retailer Zappos, computer game designer Valve and tomato-processor Morning Star, for example, have all abolished permanent managers and handed their responsibilities over to self-managing teams. Without job titles, team members flexibly adapt their roles as needed.

Mastering this new way of working takes us through different networks and identities and requires the capacity to organize oneself and others as well as to adapt to fluid hierarchies.

As such, it may be the fulfillment of Peter Drucker's organizational vision:

> … in which every man sees himself as a "manager" and accepts for himself the full burden of what is basically managerial responsibility: responsibility for his own job and work group, for his contribution to the performance and results of the entire organization, and for the social tasks of the work community.

The Gig Economy Has Given Employers More Control Over Employees' Income

Larry Elliott

Larry Elliott is the Guardian's *economics editor. He has also written seven books that focus on economic issues.*

G etting on for one million people in Britain wait each day for a text or a phone call to let them know whether an employer has work for them. Twenty years ago few had heard of zero-hour contracts, but the number of workers covered by them has increased more than fourfold since the recession of a decade ago.

During the same period underemployment—people who would work longer hours if they were available—has also increased. So has self-employment, often because someone previously employed is now scratching a living as best they can. In the 1990s, poverty was associated with workless households. Today 60% of those living below the breadline live in a household where at least one person is in work.

Language matters. There was a time when these trends would have been described as casualisation or exploitation. They would have been seen as symbolic of a one-sided labour market in which the deck was stacked in favour of employers. These days, though, it is evidence of "flexibility," and who could object to that?

The narrative goes as follows. Britain has record levels of employment and the lowest jobless rate since the mid-1970s, and that's because there are few impediments to the free market in labour. There is a reason the UK has an unemployment rate half that of France: our labour market is "flexible," the one on the other side of the Channel is "sclerotic." Employers have the confidence to hire workers because they know they can get rid of them without too much trouble. Many of the people employed on zero-hour contracts like the freedom they provide. Banning them, as the TUC is demanding, would be illiberal and economically harmful.

This argument doesn't really stack up. Britain certainly has a low unemployment rate, but so does Germany, where, despite the reforms of the early 2000s, workers have greater labour market protection. France has a higher unemployment rate, particularly for young people, but has much higher levels of productivity: GDP per head—one measure of living standards—has risen almost identically in Britain and France since 1970, a period in which the UK has deregulated its labour market, and its neighbour has not.

Britain's flexible labour market has resulted in the development of a particular sort of economy over the past decade: low productivity, low investment and low wage. Since the turn of the millennium, business investment has grown by about 1% a year on average because companies have substituted cheap workers for capital. Labour has become a commodity to be bought as cheaply as possible, which might be good for individual firms, but means people have less money to buy goods and services—a shortfall in demand only partly filled by rising levels of debt. The idea that everyone is happy with a zero-hour contract is for the birds.

Workers are cowed to an extent that has surprised the Bank of England. For years, the members of Threadneedle Street's monetary policy committee (MPC) have been expecting falling unemployment to lead to rising wage pressure, but it hasn't happened. When the financial crisis erupted in August 2007, the unemployment rate was 5.3% and annual wage growth was running at 4.7%. Today unemployment is 4.2% and earnings are growing at 2.8%.

The Bank would like to be in a position to raise interest rates, which at 0.5% are no higher today than when the economy was crashing in early 2009. For the past few months, financial markets have been softened up for a rate increase next month on the grounds that wage pressure is bubbling up. The Bank's problem is that as things stand there is a stronger case for a rate cut than a rate rise. Figures out later this week are likely to show the economy grew by just 0.2-0.3% in the first three months of the year.

The reason consumer spending is weak and the housing market is flat is that wages have not been keeping pace with inflation. In decades past, rising prices caused by a drop in the value of the pound—of the sort that the UK experienced after the EU referendum—would have been met with demands for higher wages to compensate. It didn't happen this time. Instead, the public simply accepted a period of falling living standards.

David Blanchflower, a former MPC member, says that almost a decade after the recession people remain fearful. "In the gig economy they fear that they are going to lose their jobs. Other groups of workers fear that if they ask for higher wages, the employer will bring in workers from Poland or farm everything out overseas."

This all sounds entirely plausible and fits much better with the post-recession performance of the economy than the Bank's ever-present belief that a surge in wage growth is imminent. Blanchflower says that involuntary part-time employment rose in every developed country during the financial crisis and remains above pre-recession levels. Wage inflation won't start to build until unemployment comes down a lot further, to about 3%, he suspects.

Curbs on the activities of trade unions, along with globalisation, meant the balance of power in the labour market was swinging in favour of employers long before the banks almost went bust in 2008. In previous economic cycles, a steady fall in the level of unemployment would have tilted things in the opposite direction because a shortage of available labour would have forced employers to offer higher wages.

Instead, this time the unchecked growth of the gig economy, weak enforcement of labour market regulations, a tax treatment that provides incentives for employers to hire self-employed workers, and pay restraint in the public sector explain why the past 10 years have seen the weakest real wage growth since just after the Napoleonic war. For workers life is not sweet. It was sweeter when labour markets were less flexible.

Companies in the Gig Economy Function on Manipulation

Abbey Stemler, Joshua E. Perry, and Todd Haugh

Abbey Stemler and Todd Haugh are assistant professors of business law and ethics at Indiana University. Joshua E. Perry is an associate professor of business law and ethics at Indiana University.

Uber's business model is incredibly simple: It's a platform that facilitates exchanges between people. And Uber's been incredibly successful at it, almost eliminating the transaction costs of doing business in everything from shuttling people around town to delivering food.

This is one of the reasons Uber is now among the most valuable companies in the world after its shares began trading on the New York Stock Exchange on May 10.

Yet its US$82.4 billion market capitalization may pale in comparison to the wealth of user data it's accumulating. If you use Uber—or perhaps even if you don't—it knows a treasure trove of data about you, including your location, gender, spending history, contacts, phone battery level and even whether you're on the way home from a one-night stand. It may soon know whether you're drunk or not.

While that's scary enough, combine all that data with Uber's expertise at analyzing it through the lens of behavioral science and you have a dangerous potential to exploit users for profit.

Uber's hardly alone. Our research shows the biggest digital platforms—Airbnb, Facebook, eBay and others—are collecting so much data on how we live, that they already have the capability to manipulate their users on a grand scale. They can predict behavior and influence our decisions on where to click, share and spend.

While most platforms aren't using all these capabilities yet, manipulation through behavioral psychology techniques can occur quietly and leave little trace. If we don't establish rules of the road now, it'll be much harder to detect and stop later.

"Choice Architecture"

A platform can be any space that facilitates transactions between buyers and sellers. Traditional examples include flea markets and trading floors.

A digital platform serves the same purpose but gives the owner the ability to "mediate" its users while they're using it—and often when they're not. By that we mean it can observe and learn an incredible amount of information about user behavior in order to perfect what behavioral scientists call "choice architectures," inconspicuous design elements intended to influence human behavior through how decisions are presented.

For example, Uber has experimented with its drivers to determine the most effective strategies for keeping them on the road as long as possible. These strategies include playing into cognitive biases such as loss aversion and overestimating low probability events, even if a driver is barely earning enough money to make it worth her while. Drivers end up like gamblers at a casino, urged to play just a little longer despite the odds.

Uber didn't immediately respond to a request for comment.

Airbnb also experiments with its users. It has used behavioral science to get hosts to lower their rates and accept bookings without screening guests—which creates real risks for hosts, particularly when they are sharing their own apartment.

While these examples seem relatively benign, they demonstrate how digital platforms are able to quietly design systems to direct users' actions in potentially manipulative ways.

And as platforms grow, they only become better choice architects. With its IPO's huge influx of investor money to fund more data and behavioral science, Uber could move into dangerously unethical territory—easy to imagine given its past practices.

For example, if the app recognizes that you are drunk or in a neighborhood you rarely travel to—and one that its data show is high in crime—it could charge you a higher rate, knowing you're unlikely to refuse.

Legal Challenges

And it's not all speculation.

In an effort to deceive law enforcement trying to investigate the company, Uber actually found a way to identify government regulators trying to use its app and then prevented them from getting rides.

That's one reason lawmakers and regulators have been discussing the difficult, interrelated roles of behavioral science and tech for years. And some companies, Uber in particular, have been investigated for a host of bad business practices, from discrimination to misusing user data.

But most of the manipulation we've identified and worry about is not expressly illegal. And because regulators are often unable to keep pace with the ever-evolving use of technology and choice architecture, that's likely to remain so.

Given the absence of well-defined and enforceable legal guardrails, platform companies' propensity to exploit behavioral science at users' expense will remain largely unchecked.

An Ethical Code

One solution, in our view, is establishing an ethical code for platform companies to follow. And if they don't adopt it willingly, investors, employees and users could demand it.

Since the mid-20th century, written codes of ethical conduct have been a staple of US companies. The legal and medical professions have relied on them for millennia. And research suggests they are effective at encouraging ethical behavior at companies.

We reviewed hundreds of ethical codes, including ones targeted at tech and computing companies. Based on our research, we urge digital platforms to adopt five ethical guidelines:

1. All choice architecture employed on a platform should be fully transparent. Platforms should disclose when they are using the tools of behavioral science to influence user behavior

2. Users should be able to make choices on the platform freely and easily, and choice architects should limit behavioral interventions to reminders or prompts that are the least harmful to user autonomy

3. Platforms should avoid "nudging" users in ways that exploit unconscious and irrational decision making based on impulse and emotion. New research shows that transparent choice architecture can work just as well

4. Platforms should recognize the power they possess and take care not to exploit the markets they've created, including by abusing information asymmetries between themselves and users or opposing reasonable regulations

5. Platforms should avoid using choice architecture that discourages users from acting in their own best interests. As Nobel Prize-winning behavioral economist Richard Thaler put it, we should only "nudge for good."

Big tech and behavioral science are now integrated in ways that are making companies wildly successful, from buzzing toothbrushes that make cleaning your teeth seem rewarding to using texts to nudge poorer mothers to use health care.

While the results can significantly enhance our lives, it also makes it easier than ever for companies to manipulate users to enhance their bottom lines.

Companies in the Gig Economy Are Resistant to Offering Sustainable Conditions

Levi Sumagaysay and Ethan Baron

Levi Sumagaysay is a tech reporter and editor for the Mercury News. *Ethan Baron is a business reporter at the* Mercury News.

A bill that could wreak havoc on the business models of Uber, Lyft and other companies that rely on gig workers is closer to becoming law after the California Senate passed it 29-11 along party lines Tuesday, and the state Assembly approved it by a 56-15 vote Wednesday. If signed into law, AB 5 would force firms using independent contractors to classify more of them as employees. Uber on Wednesday said it would not reclassify its drivers as employees if the bill becomes law.

The bill now goes to Gov. Gavin Newsom's desk. He is expected to sign the bill—which the San Francisco ride-hailing giants and other companies have been furiously battling against — into law after indicating his support for it in a Labor Day op-ed.

The bill was introduced by Assemblywoman Lorena Gonzalez, D-San Diego, after a sweeping State Supreme Court decision last year in a case involving delivery drivers for Dynamex, a Southern California company. The decision simplified the test for when a worker should be considered an employee. If enacted into law, AB 5 would require companies to provide a minimum wage and benefits to workers legally deemed employees, a blow for Uber and Lyft, plus startups such as food deliverer DoorDash, which have built their businesses off on-demand services provided by workers whom the companies say value the flexibility of working when they are summoned by mobile app.

"The State Senate made it clear: Your business cannot game the system by misclassifying its workers," Gonzalez said in a statement late Tuesday. "As lawmakers, we will not in good conscience allow free-riding businesses to continue to pass their own business costs onto taxpayers and workers."

Labor unions and drivers groups cheered the Senate vote.

"This is a huge win for workers across the nation!" tweeted the California Labor Federation. "It's time to rebuild the middle class and ensure all workers have the basic protections they deserve."

Uber on Wednesday pledged to keep fighting AB 5's designation of most gig-economy drivers as employees rather than independent contractors, saying it would not reclassify its drivers if the bill becomes law in January.

Uber believes its drivers qualify as independent contractors under AB 5, which would impose a three-pronged test to determine classification.

"Just because the test is hard doesn't mean we won't be able to pass it," Uber's chief legal officer Tony West said in a press call. "We continue to believe that drivers are properly classified as independent. At the end of the day, a third party—a judge or an arbitrator—will make that decision. Uber is no stranger to legal battles."

To pass AB 5's test, a company would have to show that a worker was free from control and direction by the "hiring entity," that the work was outside the the usual course of the entity's business, and that the worker was "customarily engaged in an independently established trade, occupation, or business of the same nature as the work performed."

West pointed to drivers' flexible hours, schedules and locations, and their freedom to work for other app-based firms as examples of drivers' independence from the company.

Regarding Uber's usual course of business, West described the company as a "technology platform for several different types of digital marketplaces" rather than just a transportation service.

The Bay Area Council, composed of CEOs and top executives from the region's biggest companies, also expressed disappointment. Spokesman Rufus Jeffries said Wednesday that it would be "a huge blow to California's innovation economy." The council urged Newsom to reconsider his support.

Lyft last week pointed to a Beacon Economics report that predicts more than 300,000 of its drivers would be put out of work unless they are allowed to remain independent contractors.

Gig Workers Rising, a group that has helped organize drivers' actions to advocate for the bill, called that fear-mongering.

"Let's be clear: Uber and Lyft's threats to lay off workers because of AB 5 are the same sort of classic intimidation tactics used by anti-worker corporations," Shona Clarkson, an organizer for the group, said Wednesday. "Drivers are the foundation of these companies—and without them, they're nothing."

Even if the bill is signed by Newsom, the battle over worker classification would be far from over. Uber, Lyft and DoorDash recently said they are putting a combined $90 million into a campaign for a measure that would bring the issue before California voters. The companies are offering concessions, such as a minimum wage, but they still don't want their workers to be classified as employees.

"We are fully prepared to take this issue to the voters of California to preserve the freedom and access drivers and riders want and need," a Lyft spokesman said Tuesday night.

But the companies are free to provide drivers "with some sort of flexibility, which could take a number of different forms," said William Gould IV, emeritus professor of law at Stanford Law School and a former chief of the National Labor Relations Board. "As a matter of law, an employee can have flexible hours."

A DoorDash spokeswoman sent a statement, which read in part, "DoorDash is committed to passing a new law—in the legislature or at the ballot—that would create benefits and protections for Dashers."

Beth Ross, a longtime labor attorney based in San Francisco, pointed out that the ride-hailing giants will be unable to bring the issue before voters before the law is set to take effect in January.

"They will be in a pickle," she said Wednesday. Besides having to pay minimum wage and overtime, she said the companies might be liable under the expense-reimbursement statute, meaning they'd have to pay costs drivers incur as part of their duties. Assembly Bill 5 also would give big cities the right to sue companies for non-compliance.

"We're in a whole new world," she added. "It's very much in the hands of the affected companies to restructure in a way that allows them to operate like they have."

Ross also said other companies that rely on contract workers, such as those that provide truck delivery services, are likely to take legal action.

Meanwhile, newspaper publishers had come out against AB 5, saying it would affect their struggling businesses if they have to classify newspaper carriers as employees. Gonzalez agreed to a companion measure, AB 170, which would grant publishers a one-year delay for compliance with AB 5, the Los Angeles Times reported.

Shares of Uber and Lyft were higher Wednesday. Some analysts predicted the companies would adjust to what could be their new reality.

"We expect Uber, Lyft, and other gig economy companies will reduce hiring and reduce flexibility of its workforce in California, offsetting the positive protection measures drivers will get," said Dan Ives, of Wedbush Securities, in a note to clients.

CHAPTER 3

Should the Gig Economy Be More Regulated?

Regulating the Gig Economy Requires Balancing Priorities

The World Bank Group

The World Bank is a global financial institution that provides loans and grants to the governments of developing countries to pursue capital projects.

By some measures, 40% of US workers will be in non-standard jobs by the year 2020. These could be a series of part time roles, or as a freelance contractor working via a technology platform such as Uber. In the developing world, these forms of employment are also increasing at a time when the push to move employment from the informal to the formal sector is gathering pace. The great question is therefore how do you regulate these working arrangements? How do you find the right balance between protecting workers and allowing companies the flexibility to make HR decisions?

The fact is these types of non-standard employment contract are becoming more prevalent, rather than less. In 2012, 11.8% of the workers in OECD countries had temporary contracts. This rises to 26.9 % in Poland, 23.6% in Spain, 20.7% in Portugal, and 13.7% in Japan. These temporary contracts typically come with less protection, fewer benefits and pecuniary discounts. Temporary workers in the EU earn on average 14% less than workers with open-ended contracts.

This atomization of work is a fact of life for many workers, whether they are in the developing or the developed world. "It is absolutely a trend that we need to acknowledge," says Arup Banerji, Senior Director of the Social Protection and Labor Global Practice at the World Bank in Washington, DC. "Anything that can be made piecemeal and opened up will be. Work is not being done in fixed units anymore. It is being shared and this allows more and more people to enter the work place. But how can these workers be protected?"

Without changes to regulations, this army of freelancers, subcontractors and piece workers will be left out of the traditional social protection systems such as unemployment benefits, sick pay and pensions. One of the key recommendations from a new report recently issued by the World Bank, in conjunction with the International Labor Organization (ILO), is that countries need to extend their social and labor protections to people who are working part time or in serial part time or temporary jobs.

The key to making this happen could be to use the very same technology that is being used to drive the gig economy. "There is huge scope for governments to use technology for enforcing the new regulations," says Sandra Polaski, Deputy-Director General of policy for the ILO. "Most transactions on the gig economy are done via the internet and as such they can be tracked. These companies do need to contribute to insurance and other social contributions."

While the gig economy can be beneficial for some firms and some workers, it can be detrimental to society and the economy as a whole. Peter Bakvis, the Washington Director of the International Trade Union Confederation (ITUC), notes that since the global financial crisis of 2008-2009, 30 million people have lost their jobs and wages have not kept up with productivity growth. "This is not due to over-regulation," he says. "There has been a weakening of labor market standards." He points out that increasingly complex supply chains and sub-contracting make it hard to enforce protections. But without doing so we will not be able to combat the increasing levels of inequality. "It has gone too far in some cases and we need to work with countries to establish the right levels of regulations."

Polaski is skeptical about whether the gig economy really is a new way of working. Rather, many people who are working this way are actually employees in disguise. As such the employers are not paying the true costs for employing them. "The gig economy is a way of externalizing costs," she says. "In other words it allows some sectors of society not to pay the true costs for making profits."

The best way to ensure that society as a whole does not pay the costs of the gig economy is to extend labor market regulations to everyone. "There should be a guiding principle that the architecture of labor market regulations should aim for equal treatment of all workers whatever their type of contracts," says Carmen Pages-Serra, Chief of Labor Markets at the Inter-American Development Bank. "But that is easier said than done. Much of the existing legislation is still based on people having a salaried job. But if contractors are actually contented entrepreneurs, we must be very careful not to crush this movement by over-regulation." The key to find the right balance is to ensure that there is a social dialogue between all the relevant parties.

- Employment contracts should ensure adequate protection for all workers, independent of the type of employment contract.
- Legislation should treat workers in temporary or part-time employment to protection equivalent to that of comparable permanent full-time workers.
- Employers should facilitate atypical workers' access to appropriate training opportunities to enhance their skills, career development, and occupational mobility.
- Equalizing benefits and dismissal procedures between fixed-term and open-ended contracts might prevent misuse of successive fixed-term contracts.
- Employers should also inform fixed-term workers about vacancies that become available to ensure that they have the same opportunity to secure permanent positions as other workers.
- It is important to allow the inclusion of a probationary period in the employment contract to confirm that the employee has the necessary professional and social skills.
- To prevent abuse of the probationary period, it might be appropriate to set a maximum number of trial workers for a single position.

The Gig Economy Has Not Been Open to Regulations That Would Benefit Workers and Consumers

Corporate Europe Observatory

The Corporate Europe Observatory (CEO) is a Brussels-based research organization focused on the effects of corporate lobbying in the EU.

As gig economy companies are spending more than ever on lobbying the EU, a new study today shows how the likes of Uber and AirBnB are fighting the regulation of their sector in Europe. "Uber Influential" reveals lobbying tactics of the billion-dollar corporations, whose business depends on the exemption from social and workers' rights laws, as well as the tax rules that apply to their analogue competitors.

Across Europe, an estimated 10% of the workforce are now earning some of their income with the help of tech solutions provided by gig economy companies. But the rapid rise of the gig economy and its companies is based on their systematic lobbying to avert any meaningful regulation of the sector, Corporate Europe Observatory and the Austrian Chamber of Labour warn in this latest publication.

The platform companies' strategy has found fertile ground at the European Commission. A rather single-minded view of the corporate "sharing economy" championed by Uber, Airbnb, Deliveroo, TaskRabbit and others has led the institution to assist platforms in fighting any attempt to control their operations.

In Brussels, these platform companies have in recent years intensified their lobbying to remain exempt from the EU's E-Commerce Directive and its Services Directive and thus escape regulation at regional, national and EU levels. This has exacerbated

"Gig economy lobbies fight regulation, as workers and consumers pay the price," Corporate Europe Observatory, May 9, 2019. Reprinted by permission.

the precarious situation of the sectors' workers and is eroding social rights across the EU.

Connecting the dots between these big regulatory blind spots and the sector's fast increasing activities in Brussels, "Uber Influential" provides a compelling glimpse into the tactics and consequences of coordinated EU lobbying efforts by a novel industry receiving European Commission help to avoid regulation—at the expense of EU citizens.

Corporate Europe Observatory's researcher and campaigner Kenneth Haar said:

> "There is a need for a new European approach to the platform economy. Creating a safe haven for huge companies such as Uber and Airbnb to escape the rules others have to follow is grotesque and comes at a high price for workers, consumers, and analogue competitors. Politicians across Europe have to take control over gig economy rules, and end the laissez-faire modus of the Commission and the courts we've been seeing."

Frank Ey, expert on EU affairs at the Austrian Chamber of Labour added:

> "The new EU Commission must show more respect for workers' rights and the interests of the general public rather than only listening to business lobbyists. Technological innovation should no longer be used as a pretext for creating new precarious working conditions, and digitalisation mustn't serve as a buzzword to whitewash the erosion of labour and social rights or tax evasion."

The Gig Economy Presents Economic Risks for Those Who Participate in It

Sarah Kaine and Emmanuel Josserand

Sarah Kaine is an associate professor in the UTS Centre for Business and Social Innovation at the University of Technology Sydney. Emmanuel Josserand is a professor of management and Director of the Centre for Business and Social Innovation at the University of Technology Sydney.

To secure work in the gig economy, workers often have to contribute not just their time and labour but also their capital. This means workers are not only shouldering the risks associated with insecure employment but also the risks associated with investing capital into businesses which they have little control over.

In the traditional economy businesses provide capital and employees provide labour. This is being challenged by the disruption wrought by technology, specifically the multitude of digital matching platforms.

There are now a vast array of organisations providing very different goods and services using digital platforms to match consumers and service providers in the sharing economy (also known as the collaborative economy, access economy or peer economy).

In this type of economy many organisations are "asset light." This means businesses make money through providing access to goods and services and making connections between smaller providers and consumers. In doing so, the risk shifts from business to individual gig workers.

In its recently released report into digital disruption, the Productivity Commission described gig work as a model of hiring labour on demand. This is facilitated through platform websites (think Uber, TaskRabbit, Amazon Mechanical Turk), enabling work to be broken down into components which allows tasks to be allocated as needed. The Commission's report warns that while "gigging" might increase flexibility of work it means workers bear more risk because of fragmented, insecure employment.

Gig workers are increasingly taking risks related not only to their labour but also to their own capital. This occurs when continued ownership of the assets used in work are dependent on a set of circumstances outside the control of the worker. For example, Uber drivers are encouraged to borrow money to buy their cars. If a driver is then "decommissioned" by Uber or if Uber changes the amount it pays to drivers or if the market gets flooded with new Uber drivers due to the accessibility of the platform, the driver is burdened with debt, with no ready means to pay it back.

This scenario also means that the official classification of gig workers is also contested. In the absence of a classification, gig worker status is being worked out on a case by case basis by the courts. For example the recent high profile legal cases involving Uber workers.

For platform providers there is a huge incentive to ensure their workers are not classified as employees in any sense – otherwise they would be liable for providing entitlements to workers, driving up their costs. It would also question the legitimacy of having "employees" provide the physical assets that the platform relies on to carry out its business.

The key claim of the platform providers is that their gig workers should be considered independent contractors, not employees at all. Contractors in the traditional economy, such as truck drivers, have also sometimes supplied their own "tools" but the gig economy differs in that the gig worker doesn't accumulate any goodwill that can be on-sold or leveraged for financial gain. The goodwill accrues to the platform provider, leaving the worker with fewer options.

Australia's industrial relations system seems ill-equipped to regulate for emerging forms of work, given that it continues to struggle to define long-established forms of contingent employment (such as casual work). In terms of determining if a worker is an "independent contractor" Australian courts consider whether the hirer controls the work performed; whether the worker is integrated into the hirer's organisation or is in business on their own; whether the worker is paid according to tasks completed or time spent working and whether the worker can subcontract out work, or is free to work for other hirers.

For example, bicycle couriers and insurance agents have been found by the courts to be employees because they were subject to hirer instructions or could not be said to be in business on their own. But in the absence of further regulation, each situation has to be assessed and tested on a case-by-case basis—a piecemeal and time consuming approach.

As the gigging economy gains momentum, policymakers, labour activists and the media are asking questions about how we conceptualise work and protect workers.

The experience of labour regulation in supply chains provides some indication about what may happen in the gig economy space—specifically that economically dominant agents (a common example being big retailers or other quasi-monopolies) set the rules. That companies with global footprints are able to influence political contexts, obscure lines of liability, and restructure out risk. Early indications by big players like Uber demonstrate they have observed and learnt these lessons too.

To provide protections to workers in the gig economy Australia is going to have to grapple with these questions and with a reality in which workers don't just provide labour but also capital, absorbing more business risk than ever.

Under Self-Regulation, Companies in the Gig Economy Operate Legally but Not in an Economically Secure Way

Genevieve Shanahan and Mark Smith

Genevieve Shanahan is a research assistant and PhD candidate at Grenoble École de Management in France. Mark Smith is the Dean of Faculty and a professor of human resource management at Grenoble École de Management.

In Europe and around the world, many people are delivering fast food on bicycles or acting as taxi drivers in their own cars, not quite employees and not quite self-employed. Following recent legal judgements in France, the UK and in other countries, the contractual status of these "gig workers" is again being questioned. We hear of the benefits of the flexible lifestyles afforded to workers in the "gig economy" but also complaints about precariousness and exploitation.

While gig economy platforms might be behaving in accordance with their legal contracts, many workers appear to feel that they are not being treated fairly. Another form of contract—known as the "psychological contract"—can perhaps help us understand.

Who Is Working in the Gig Economy?

All the signs suggest continued growth in the gig economy—paid work in short spells with no or limited commitment from either worker or company. This work frequently involves driving and delivering but can also cover other platform-mediated, short-term work, such as data coding. The work is frequently associated with the young—one survey in North America found that over 70% were aged under 45 and 90% were in higher education.

This youth profile allows proponents of gig work to justify the limited level of security, providing access to work for people with limited professional experience. Furthermore, having another activity, such as being a student, makes the flexibility and autonomy attractive.

Yet such on-demand service work leads to a rise in precariousness more generally, and may increase difficulties for finding secure, full-time work. Recent EU research highlights how damaging this "bogus self-employment" can be for young people trying to start their careers. Here we can see parallels with other forms of precarious work, such as temporary and zero-hour contracts, that are similarly prevalent among young people.

Tensions in the Gig Economy

Across various platforms of the gig economy, workers are agitating for more. There is evidence of Uber drivers wanting the right to unionise and some Foodora riders want their platform to pay operational costs, such as bike maintenance and mobile data fees. Workers on Amazon Mechanical Turk have petitioned to be treated like humans, not algorithms.

Many focus their complaints around a desire to be treated as employees. They claim to have the obligations of employees but not the benefits. Yet gig platforms are clear that they do not recognise this employee status nor the obligations that would come with such a relationship.

Violating the "Psychological Contract"

One way of understanding these tensions is through the lens of "psychological contracts." Human resource management theorists have developed this concept to describe the various unwritten agreements, both explicit and implicit, that workers and employers believe they have with one another. It captures the intangible and hard to quantify elements of the employer-employee relationship, beyond the legal contract. These elements can include considerations of flexibility in the scope of the work, use of initiative, evolution of roles and workers' loyalty to the employer.

These psychological contracts function when they are more or less balanced. The employee and employer make commitments to one another that make the relationship attractive to both parties. The ongoing nature of the relationship allows trust and reciprocity to develop.

Gig Platforms Say They Want a One-Night Stand, Not a Relationship

Of course, not all employment relationships are ongoing. Psychological contract theory tells us that gig work, like other types of short-term work relationships, will tend to be more "transactional" rather than "relational," with more straightforward exchange and less focus on mutual trust and commitment.

The latter seems to capture the relationship the gig economy platforms wish to foster, particularly in light of claims by platform workers to be employees. The platforms have tailored the terms and language of their contracts in order to demand a minimum of their workers and justify minimal obligations in return. Indeed for some workers, these transactional contracts are ideal.

A Rough Deal, or A Broken One?

Yet protests and legal actions show that not all workers are happy. Psychological contract theory might offer two potential explanations for the tensions of the gig economy—workers are unhappy with the terms of the psychological contract, or they believe the platforms have violated the contract.

It is clear that some workers find the terms unfair. While it might be argued that workers have consented to these terms, consent becomes problematic when there are few better options. Young people in some countries face a lack of jobs, pushing them into low quality, poorly paid and precarious gig work.

It is also possible that gig workers initially consent to the psychological contract, but then believe the platform violates the terms. For instance, in 2016 Deliveroo encouraged workers to move to a new service contract, claiming that it would work out better for riders—when some found insufficient volume of work to maintain their earnings, the psychological contract was arguably violated.

A Perception of Reciprocity

Perception is an important feature of psychological contracts and the perceptions of the worker and firm are not necessarily always aligned. Since the terms of such psychological contracts are "in the eye of the beholder," one party can believe that the other is failing to live up to obligations that the other does not recognise.

These perceptions can be informed by the legal and social context, and notions of what is fair. For example, ongoing research at Grenoble Ecole de Management has found that delivery riders perceive good customer service, such as rectifying errors, to be part of the job, yet they are not paid for such additional tasks. The platforms benefit from this commitment. On the other side, gig workers often expect, based on common-sense ideas of fairness, that platforms would not deactivate an account due to unreasonable passenger ratings. When this happens, the sense of betrayal can be intense. Reciprocity is what makes more conventional employer-employee relationships function and is perhaps part of what is missing for gig workers today.

The Current Gig Economy Benefits Businesses, Not Employees

Charlotte Pickles

Charlotte Pickles is the director of Reform, an independent, nonpartisan think tank focused on improving public services that is based in the United Kingdom. She was formerly the managing editor at Unherd.

C ontorted, indecipherable and window-dressing," that's how Judge Joanna Wade described delivery service CitySprint's contractual arrangements with its couriers.[1] The case, in which a London employment tribunal found that CitySprint should have treated a cycle courier as a worker rather than an independent contractor, is one of a flurry being brought against gig economy platforms.

Uber never seems to be out of the courts. In America, eleven cases are currently sitting with the 9th US Circuit Court of Appeals. In the UK, the ride-hailing company looks set for a trip to the Supreme Court in its fight against a tribunal ruling that its drivers should be classified as workers.

The plight of gig workers has become the *cause celebre* of workers' rights. Greedy gig platforms are condemned as the modern-day equivalent of the exploitative factory owners of the industrial revolution. Sick pay? The minimum wage? Bargaining rights? Not for the "gigger." Instead there's flexibility and control—which, the companies argue—is why people sign up.

The CitySprint case was brought by a single employee, but as with those against Uber, the implications are sector-wide. As this model matures, the relevant companies will need to make changes. The greater concern should be the spread of gig-style labour models to non-gig work—and we're already seeing that happen.

The Gig Economy Works for Many

Companies arguing that workers want flexibility are not wrong:

- Detailed research by the RSA think tank found that more than half of UK gig workers viewed the work positively, citing advantages like flexibility or decent pay; and 63% of current workers agreed that it allowed them to have more "control and freedom over when they work".[2]
- A McKinsey report looking at America and Europe found that the majority of gig workers are independent contractors by choice.[3] They also found that for every worker whose primary earnings are from contracting, but would prefer a traditional job, more than two traditional workers would like to become independent contractors.

The controversy engulfing the gig model risks undermining what makes gig work so attractive to so many.

And it risks ignoring the broader benefits that disruptive app-based companies such as Uber, TaskRabbit and Handy are delivering—making services cheaper and more accessible for consumers; directly connecting service providers with their market, in real time; and lowering the barriers to entry for people seeking employment, particularly for young people.

The benefits of removing the middleman shouldn't be underestimated. There are now gig platforms for social care workers, supply teachers and health workers, cutting out the agency fees and paying higher wages. These are people who are better off because of the advent of gig platforms.

This is not to say that greater protections for workers are unwarranted. While a majority of gig workers are actively choosing that model of work—often supplementing other sources of income—a good chunk, estimated at just over a quarter in the UK and US, do so out of necessity. That is, they can't find sufficient "regularised" work elsewhere.

And while many gig platforms have developed in sectors that were already heavily skewed towards self-employment (something critics conveniently forget), that doesn't mean action shouldn't be taken to raise standards—particularly when more and more people are working in this way. Plus, strictly speaking, there is a difference between being self-employed, running your own enterprise, and being an independent contractor working for a single company.

A review of "good work," commissioned by the UK government and triggered by concerns about working conditions in the burgeoning gig economy, argues the onus should be on the companies:[4]

> "The best way to achieve better work is not national regulation but responsible corporate governance, good management and strong employment relations within the organisation, which is why it is important that companies are seen to take good work seriously and are open about their practices and that all workers are able to be engaged and heard."

The RSA recommend a "Charter for Good Work in the Gig Economy," a collaboration between government, companies and representative bodies to agree a set of standards that value workers.[5] As the gig economy grows, putting more traditional employee-based firms out of business, and disrupting new industries, it's right that businesses take seriously the economic and social security of their workers—contractors or not. A Charter would be a good place to start.

The greatest challenge, however, is the threat of the gig model being bastardised by unscrupulous businesses looking to increase profits at the expense of their workers. As a joint report by two UK parliamentary committees this week put it: "willingness to exploit workers should not be a competitive advantage."[6]

It's called the gig economy for a reason—workers get paid for discrete "gigs," like hanging a picture, developing an app, cleaning a flat; and they perform multiple gigs for multiple clients. That's why it's a form of self-employment. And why self-employment and employment are treated differently. Blurring those lines to cut costs is a cynical move that makes a mockery of the age-old "social contract" between business, workers and the state.

We can already see it happening.

Take budget airline Ryanair for example, recently in the news for cancelling thousands of flights. Ryanair uses "self-employed" pilots, thereby enabling them to avoid employee-related taxes and benefits.

Writing in *The New York Times* Liz Alderman and Amie Tsang report on conditions at Ryanair similar to those experienced by gig workers at companies such as Uber and Deliveroo: pilots and crew say they only get paid for flight time, not preparation; their hours are not guaranteed; and they have to cover their own, unavoidable, expenses such as hotels and transport, even their own uniforms.[7]

Unlike genuine gig workers, however, Ryanair pilots are not undertaking "gigs." They work for one company, on that company's schedule—how is that different from an employee? If the trade made by self-employed people is flexibility and control in exchange for fewer benefits, Ryanair pilots are getting all of the downside and none of the upside.

The greatest challenge is the threat of the gig model being bastardised by unscrupulous businesses looking to increase profits at the expense of their workers. As a joint report by two UK parliamentary committees this week put it: "willingness to exploit workers should not be a competitive advantage."

What happens when Ryanair is no longer an outlier but the norm? That's not so difficult to imagine. The rise of the actual gig economy has been swift, and we didn't see it coming.

Management consultancy firms could decide to make their consultants contractors, and their HQs the "platform" for allocating labour. Major retailers could start allocating shifts as 'gig' work — the next step from zero hour contracts? A major hotel chain could start getting housekeeping or reception services on a flexible, as-needed basis. Or a factory starts contracting assembly line workers according to the ebb and flow of orders.

That's a level of disruption no economy or society is prepared for, and one that requires an entirely new approach to tax and social security.

The two UK parliamentary committees warning of the risks of exploitative behaviour have gone so far as to draft legislation which, if enacted, would introduce "a new presumption of 'worker by default' that would require companies to provide basic safety net standards of rights and benefits to their workers—or prove that their working practices are genuinely reflecting of self-employment."[8]

Such a measure will undoubtedly raise the heckles of businesses and their trade body cheerleaders. They will call it heavy-handed; burdensome regulation that stifles innovation. But if employers continue pushing at the limits of what society deems fair and decent, if they rip up the social contract, then they shouldn't be surprised when society pushes back.

References

1. "Courier wins holiday pay in key tribunal ruling on gig economy," The Guardian, 6 January 2017

2. Brhmie Balaram, Josie Warden and Fabian Wallace-Stephens, "Good Gigs. A fairer future for the UK's gig economy," RSA, April 2017

3. "Independent work. Choice, necessity and the gig economy," McKinsey Global Institute, October 2016

4. "Good work: the Taylor review of modern working practices," 11 July 2017

5. Brhmie Balaram, Josie Warden and Fabian Wallace-Stephens, "Good Gigs. A fairer future for the UK's gig economy," RSA, April 2017

6. *A framework for modern employment*, Second Report of the Work and Pensions Committee and First Report of the Business, Energy and Industrial Strategy Committee of Session 2017–19, 15 November 2017

7. Liz Alderman and Amie Tsang, "Jet Pilot Might Not Seem Like a 'Gig,' but at Ryanair, It Is," *The New York Times*, 16 November 2017

8. "Committees publish bill to end exploitation," Work and Pensions and Business, Energy and Industrial Strategy Committees, 20 November 2017

Self-Regulation Can Be an Effective Tool to Protect the Rights of Workers and Companies

Scott Shackelford

Scott Shackelford is an associate professor at the Indiana University Kelley School of Business.

I f Boeing is allowed to certify that a crash-prone aircraft is safe, and Facebook can violate users' privacy expectations, should companies and industries ever be allowed to police themselves? The debate is heating up particularly in the US tech sector with growing calls to regulate—or even break up—the likes of Google, Apple and Amazon.

It turns out to be possible, at least sometimes, for companies and industries to govern themselves, while still protecting the public interest. Groundbreaking work by Nobel Prize-winning political economist Elinor Ostrom and her husband Vincent found a solution to a classic economic quandary, in which people—and businesses—self-interestedly enrich themselves as quickly as possible with certain resources including personal data, thinking little about the secondary costs they might be inflicting on others.

As the director of the Ostrom Workshop Program on Cybersecurity and Internet Governance, I have been involved in numerous projects studying how to solve these sorts of problems when they arise, both online and offline. Most recently, my work has looked at how to manage the massively interconnected world of sensors, computers and smart devices—what I and others call the "internet of everything."

I've found that there are ways companies can become leaders by experimenting with business opportunities and collaborating with peers, while still working with regulators to protect the public, including both in the air and in cyberspace.

Tragedy Revisited

In a classic economic problem, called "the tragedy of the commons," a parcel of grassland is made available for a community to graze its livestock. Everyone tries to get the most benefit from it—and as a result, the land is overgrazed. What started as a resource for everyone becomes of little use to anyone.

For many years, economists thought there were only two possible solutions. One was for the government to step in and limit how many people could graze their animals. The other was to split the land up among private owners who had exclusive use of it, and could sustainably manage it for their individual benefit.

The Ostroms, however, found a third way. In some cases, they revealed, self-organization can work well, especially when the various people and groups involve can communicate effectively. They called it "polycentric governance," because it allows regulation to come from more than just one central authority. Their work can help determine if and when companies can effectively regulate themselves—or whether it's best for the government to step in.

A Polycentric Primer

The concept can seem complicated, but in practice it is increasingly popular, in federal programs and even as a goal for governing the internet.

Scholars such as Elinor Ostrom produced a broad swath of research over decades, looking at public schools and police department performance in Midwestern US cities, coastal overfishing, forest management in nations like Nepal, and even traffic jams in New York City. They identified commonalities among all these studies, including whether the group's members can help set the rules by which their shared resources are governed, how much control they have over who gets to share it, how disputes are resolved, and how everyone's use is monitored.

All of these factors can help predict whether individuals or groups will successfully self-regulate, whether the challenge they're facing is climate change, cybersecurity, or anything else. Trust is key, as Lin Ostrom said, and an excellent way to build trust is to let smaller groups make their own decisions.

Polycentric governance's embrace of self-regulation involves relying on human ingenuity and collaboration skills to solve difficult problems—while focusing on practical measures to address specific challenges.

Self-regulation does have its limits, though—as has been clear in the revelations about how the Federal Aviation Administration allowed Boeing to certify the safety of its own software. Facebook has also been heavily criticized for failing to block an anonymous horde of users across the globe from manipulating people's political views.

Polycentric regulation is a departure from the idea of "keep it simple, stupid"—rather, it is a call for engagement by numerous groups to grapple with the complexities of the real world.

Both Facebook and Boeing now need to convince themselves, their employees, investors, policymakers, users and customers that they can be trusted. Ostrom's ideas suggest they could begin to do this by engaging with peers and industry groups to set rules and ensure they are enforced.

Governing the 'Internet of Everything'

Another industry in serious need of better regulations is the smart-device business, with tens of billions of connected devices around the world, and little to no concern for user security or privacy.

Customers often buy the cheapest smart-home camera or digital sensor, without looking at competitors' security and privacy protections. The results are predictable—hackers have hijacked thousands of internet-connected devices and used them to attack the physical network of the internet, take control of industrial equipment, and spy on private citizens through their smartphones and baby monitors.

Some governments are starting to get involved. The state of California and the European Union are exploring laws that promote "reasonable" security requirements, at least as a baseline. The EU is encouraging companies to band together to establish industry-wide codes of conduct.

Getting Governance Right

Effective self-governance may seem impossible in the "Internet of everything" because of the scale and variety of groups and industries involved, but polycentric governance does provide a useful lens through which to view these problems. Ostrom has asserted this approach may be the most flexible and adaptable way to manage rapidly changing industries. It may also help avoid conflicting government regulations that risk stifling innovation in the name of protecting consumers without helping either cause.

But success is not certain. It requires active engagement by all parties, who must share a sense of responsibility to the customers and mutual trust in one another. That's not easy to build in any community, let alone the dynamic tech industry.

Government involvement can help build bridges and solidify trust across the private sector, as happened with cybersecurity efforts from the National Institute for Standards and Technology. Some states, like Ohio, are even rewarding firms for using appropriate self-regulation in their cybersecurity decision-making.

Polycentric governance can be flexible, adapting to new technologies more appropriately—and often more quickly—than pure governmental regulation. It also can be more efficient and cost-effective, though it's not a cure for all regulatory ills. And it's important to note that regulation can spur innovation as well as protect consumers, especially when the rules are simple and outcome focused.

Consider the North American Electric Reliability Council. That organization was originally created as a group of companies that came together voluntarily in an effort to protect against blackouts. NERC standards, however, were eventually made legally enforceable in the aftermath of the Northeast blackout of 2003. They are an example of an organic code of conduct that was voluntarily adopted and subsequently reinforced by government, consistent with professor Ostrom's ideas. Ideally, it should not require such a crisis to spur this process forward.

Ultimately, what's needed—and what professor Ostrom and her colleagues and successors have called for—is more experimentation and less theorizing. As the 10-year anniversary of Ostrom's Nobel Prize approaches, I believe it is time to put her insights to work, offering industries the opportunity to self-regulate where appropriate while leaving the door open for the possibility of government action, including antitrust enforcement, to protect the public and promote cyber peace.

Regulation Can Stifle Growth and Innovation in an Emerging Market

Matthew Bevan

Matthew Bevan is the host of the Australian Broadcast Company podcast Russia, If You're Listening, *and the newsreader for* RN Breakfast.

It's been an interesting year for the multinational gig economy—the loose conglomeration of companies including Uber, Deliveroo and Airtasker that connect users online with independent contractors willing to deliver something to them, drive them around, or complete miscellaneous tasks.

One of the men who started the whole craze, Uber founder Travis Kalanick, was forced to resign.

Concerns that Kalanick's win-at-all-costs mentality was harming female employees, low-income drivers and customers caused enough bad press that the all important stock price dipped, leading to a shareholder revolt.

But Uber's employees were unhappy too. Many drivers and customers left the company in protest over Kalanick's leadership and the company's love of changing terms of service and hated background checks for drivers.

Additionally, while gig economy behemoths love saying they're only thriving because of a lack of government regulation, in the UK at least, the regulators are on the way.

Earlier this month, UK Prime Minister Theresa May launched the Taylor Review into Employment Practices in the Modern Economy, led by former Labour Party heavyweight Matthew Taylor, saying its findings would help stop the exploitation of gig economy workers, without stifling innovation.

While the UK Government has not yet committed to the findings of the report, there may be lessons in it for Australia.

Senior Researcher Brhmie Balaram, from Matthew Taylor's organisation The RSA, said an important aspect of the Taylor Review was a suggestion that people in the gig economy be reclassified.

"While it should be decided on a case-by-case basis, I think that what we're trying to say is that if you classify people in the UK employment category of workers rather than independent contractors, you will be able to guarantee them a level of rights and protections such as minimum wage, holiday pay and rest breaks," she said.

Additionally, the Taylor Review recommends that some provision be given for career progression in gig economy companies.

Uber Power Over Drivers

Another issue is how much power workers have to change their conditions.

The terms of service contract Uber drivers are required to agree to is regularly changed by the company, meaning the amount of income for the same amount of work can be cut unilaterally.

For some drivers, who have invested in high-end or new model cars to improve the service they provide to their customers, this can mean a significant investment is now worthless.

According to Dr Sarah Kaine from the University of Technology Sydney Business School, gig economy companies like us to think that fixing the problem of classifying their workers is much harder than it is.

"Currently it is the companies that are deciding how to classify these workers. At the moment they're maintaining that they're independent contractors," she said.

"We do have provisions under the Fair Work Act to try and limit 'sham contracting', whereby you call workers contractors even if they're not, and the Fair Work Ombudsman is very active in trying to make sure that kind of contracting doesn't happen.

"What workers really want is to be treated fairly. They want to have a say, instead of being on the end of unilateral changes."

At the moment, this isn't an issue for most Australians, as most of us are full-time employees or casual workers.

However, in the future, it might become a much bigger problem as the number of people working in the gig economy increases.

"What happens when you have 30 or 40 per cent of workers working as quasi-independent contractors who haven't made provisions for superannuation? What happens to the tax base in that situation?" said Dr Kaine.

The UK Government appears to already be moving towards solving this problem and, as some of the shine starts to come off the multinational gig economy companies, a change may arrive in Australia too.

Regulation Would Reduce the Flexibility of Gig Work

Timothy B. Lee

Timothy B. Lee is a senior tech policy reporter for Ars Technica. *He is based in Washington, DC.*

Both houses of California's legislature have passed sweeping legislation requiring businesses to treat more of their workers as employees rather than independent contractors. As a result, more workers will enjoy protections like the minimum wage and benefits such as unemployment insurance. The bill is now on its way to Governor Gavin Newsom, who is expected to sign it.

The law will apply across the California economy, but it could have particularly stark consequences for Uber and Lyft—both of which are based in the Golden State. The companies currently treat their drivers as independent contractors, and their entire business model is built around that assumption.

In the hours after the legislation cleared the California legislature, Uber and Lyft both blasted the law and vowed to seek changes.

"California is missing a real opportunity to lead the nation by improving the quality, security and dignity of independent work," Uber's Tony West said. In an emailed statement, Lyft argued that the "overwhelming majority of rideshare drivers" want "a thoughtful solution that balances flexibility with an earnings standard and benefits"—a standard Lyft argues that the new legislation doesn't meet.

Uber and Lyft are still hoping that Governor Newsom will push through follow-up legislation specifically for "gig economy" workers. If that doesn't happen, Uber, Lyft, and Doordash have also vowed to spend $30 million backing a ballot initiative to overturn the law.

But if those efforts fail, then "gig economy" companies could be forced to rethink their business models. And the results may not be entirely positive for Uber and Lyft drivers.

More Workers Will Be Employees in California

Labor law draws a basic distinction between employees and independent contractors. If you're an employee, you have a boss who sets your schedule, tells you what kind of work to do, and pays you at least minimum wage. Independent contractors, on the other hand, are people who—at least theoretically—run their own, separate businesses. Think about a plumber you hire once to fix a leaky pipe, for example.

In recent years, employers have pushed the legal envelope, trying to classify as many workers as possible as independent contractors. Worker rights advocates have objected, arguing that these workers were being wrongfully denied protections they were entitled to under labor law.

One of those conflicts reached the California Supreme Court last year. A same-day delivery company called Dynamex once treated its drivers as employees, but it re-classified them as independent contractors in 2004. Some of those drivers sued, arguing that they should still be considered employees under California law.

Last year the California Supreme Court sided with the drivers, and in the process it established new, broader criteria for determining who was an employee. Under the test, a worker must be treated as an employee unless three conditions are met:

(a) The worker is free from control and direction over performance of the work; (b) the work provided is outside the usual course of the business for which the work is performed; and (c) the worker is customarily engaged in an independently established trade, occupation, or business

This simpler test means that a lot more workers will be classified as employees. But critics worried it could go too far, upending the businesses of professionals who have long operated as independent contractors.

So the California legislature passed legislation to ratify the *Dynamex* ruling while also limiting its scope. It carves out a number of exemptions—largely for high-earning professionals like lawyers, architects, engineers and accountants. People in these skilled occupations often operate their own independent firms and have significant bargaining power.

Under the new law, photographers, writers, and cartoonists can more easily be independent contractors if they sell fewer than 35 pieces to a single client in a year. If they sell more than that then they're likely to be classified as employees.

Uber, Lyft, Doordash, and other "gig economy" companies lobbied hard for a similar exemption covering their workers, but they came up short. So Uber and Lyft drivers—as well as delivery drivers for other on-demand services—may soon be legally considered employees of these companies.

Uber disputes that. In a Wednesday conference call, Uber chief legal officer Tony West argued that driving a car is "outside the usual course" of Uber's business. "Several previous rulings have found that drivers' work is outside the usual course of Uber's business, which is serving as a technology platform for several different types of digital marketplaces," West said.

For example, a Vermont official accepted that reasoning in a 2017 ruling using a legal standard similar to the one that now applies in California. But it's widely expected that courts in California won't see the issue the same way.

The New Law Could Mean Changes for Uber and Lyft Drivers

A big reason Uber and Lyft have been opposing this bill so ferociously is that their current business model doesn't fit well into conventional labor law categories.

Conventional labor law assumes that a worker goes to a job, clocks in, works, for a few hours, and then clocks out. In this model, the employer decides what work the worker should do; in exchange the worker is guaranteed to make at least minimum wage. Employers set worker schedules; to protect them, California law guarantees workers overtime pay and mandatory breaks.

By contrast, Uber and Lyft drivers have complete control over where and when they work. In this model, it's not clear that mandatory overtime pay helps workers, since workers never face pressure from the platforms to work longer hours. If platforms are forced to pay time-and-a-half for overtime hours, they may just ban drivers from working overtime.

A minimum wage guarantee is likely to trigger significant changes to the ride-sharing model. It's helpful here to look at New York City, where a $17.22 minimum wage for ride-hail drivers went into effect earlier this year.

To make a profit, Lyft needs to make sure drivers bring in at least $17.22 per hour in fares. To accomplish this, Lyft has imposed a new policy that (in the words of Harry Campbell) "prevents drivers from logging on to the company's app during periods of low demand." Under the new rules, Lyft drivers in New York "have to wait until ride requests pick up, or drive to a busier neighborhood."

Whether these changes ultimately benefit drivers is an open question. Probably it will benefit some drivers and harm others. Full-time drivers may not be affected very much, as Lyft exempts its most active drivers from these restrictions. On the other hand, the changes may be bad for part-time drivers who care more about flexible schedules than maximizing earnings.

We can expect similar changes in California if the new legislation ultimately causes drivers to be classified as employees. Companies will likely restrict how many people drive for them and where and when they can work. Workers who are able to get work may enjoy higher earnings, but they'll lose a bit of autonomy over their schedules. Meanwhile, with fewer drivers on the road, customers may see higher fares and longer wait times.

But the full implications won't be clear until the new rules make their way through the courts. Uber and Lyft aren't going to give up their current business model without a fight.

CHAPTER 4

Does the Gig Economy Fundamentally Change the Labor Market?

The Effects of the Gig Economy on the Workforce

Tom Gresham

Tom Gresham is director of news operations at VCU News, *the news site run by Virginia Commonwealth University.*

The growing contingent of freelancers, independent contractors and the self-employed in the American workforce has consumed the US business community and media in recent years, even as researchers wrestle with how to draw a clear picture of the nature of the country's teeming network of workers earning income outside the traditional employment structure. Large, multinational companies are built and fueled in some cases largely by these independent workers. Estimates of the size of those participating in the gig economy vary, but a 2018 study by Intuit predicted that 40 percent of American workers would be independent contractors of some kind by 2020.

Susan Coombes, Ph.D., associate professor of management and entrepreneurship in the Virginia Commonwealth University School of Business, has done extensive research on entrepreneurship. She shared her insight on the rise of the gig economy and its impact on working conditions.

Are we seeing a dramatic shift in the nature of the American workforce?

I would say it's a noteworthy shift, but not as dramatic as some might think. While the use of "gig economy" as a term in popular culture is somewhat recent, independent contractors, freelancers, and the self-employed have long existed in the marketplace. So, along with some trends in the growth of a market that recognizes

"Rise and grind: The growing gig economy and its impact on the American workforce," by Tom Gresham, Science X Network, June 4, 2019. Reprinted by permission.

the benefits of sharing and flexibility, we're also recognizing its presence more than before.

Also, does this percentage take into consideration to what degree someone is a "gig" worker? How do we define these "gigs?" Are workers purely independent, or is there some type of contracted (temporary) relationship? For instance, do they sustain themselves with independent contract work; or is it purely for supplementary purposes, when convenient? A recent NPR poll suggests around 40 percent of the population does contract work in addition to their main jobs. This shows that percentages are context/definition specific; so it's difficult to make absolute conclusions.

Additionally, one important aspect to consider is the impact of the 2008 recession on the job market. It's harder to find full-time work, with desirable salaries, so there are a lot of people—most of whom are millennials—who use gig work for either primary or supplementary financial purposes.

That being said, there is the rise of companies with business models (for example, ride-sharing) that are based predominantly on gig workers, so that is a spot where an interesting and perceptible shift is occurring. Many companies view these folks as independent contractors and freelancers, rather than actual employees, even though there is a direct association between the groups.

What are the biggest benefits for workers from the growing gig economy? Are there benefits for the larger economy and culture?

In many cases, it provides flexibility for these workers to supplement their current incomes/employment, or to pursue careers that might otherwise prove to be elusive.

For companies, both small and large, independent contractors can be a blessing. Some of these ventures cannot afford to hire full-time, long-term employees, but are in need of certain skill sets. Using independent contractors provides them with access to human resources, without requiring long-term resource investments.

For larger companies that utilize the independent job force, it can provide a valuable influx of relevant resources (human and intellectual) at the time they are most needed for various projects and strategies, without the long-term commitment. It helps companies be efficient and effective, to keep their own costs down while saving resources for other investments.

As far as our culture, there have always been those individuals and groups that perceive a need in the market that's not adequately addressed. Whether from an economic or social perspective, you'll find these folks providing solutions. If there's enough of a market that wants those particular solutions, you'll then see a shift (whether small or significant) toward that new/modified offering.

What are the biggest challenges for workers, especially those who attempt to be full-time freelancers? What kinds of sacrifices must they make to take this path?

Primarily, what comes to mind is a lack of security—a predictable paycheck, desirable benefits, a sense of long-term stability, etc.

There are pros and cons. It's similar to the perceived glory attributed to entrepreneurs who launch (or attempt to launch) their own ventures. There is a sort of romanticism to the idea of being a free agent, to calling your own shots. This can be a rewarding, but also precarious, position for some of these workers. For some, greater autonomy can be quite satisfying. It can provide the opportunity to call the shots—determining your work hours and the pace of work, how you define success for yourself, the identity you create for yourself.

However, what many people don't frequently recognize is that it's a grind and there are major obstacles that will regularly pop up, that there's high risk and potential for failure. Concurrently, there is also the emotional isolation that can occur when you're doing this on your own. You're not securely embedded in an organizational culture, and you know that success or failure rests squarely on your shoulders. For many people, a certain degree of affiliation with an organization provides a sense of emotional grounding and fulfillment. Also, if you're not bound to some sort of organizational contract, it may be more of a challenge to stay on task and remain productive.

Does the growing freelance workforce create problems for traditional workers? Is there a danger of working conditions and compensation suffering because organizations have access to this burgeoning pool of independent contractors?

In general, the use of independent contractors is probably not a threat to the greater workforce, but this issue can vary from company to company. In some organizations—especially those that are underperforming—the use of gig workers can save them money. It might even help some firms justify reducing their full-time, traditional workforce. It could also be a considerable issue in particular market niches (for example, the impact of ride-sharing on the taxi industry in some cities).

The issues of work conditions and compensation are also probably contingent on the specific companies and industries themselves. Overall, companies are going to be pretty consistent in the way they treat (or mistreat) their workers, and those practices aren't going to madly fluctuate based on the category of employment. If a company is known for treating its traditional employees fairly, they'll likely also follow through with this behavior regarding freelancers. On the other hand, there's little reason to think that a company known for unfair or exploitive practices would somehow improve their treatment of workers based on whether they are traditional or not.

The Gig Economy Is Fundamentally Different from the Labor Market of the Past

Shelly Strom

Shelly Strom is a writer for Liveops, a cloud contact call center based in Scottsdale, Arizona.

What does a traditional job look like? Many people would describe it as a full-time role with a single company. Yet, the FTE—full-time equivalent—employee/employer relationship is a fairly recent phenomenon. And it appears that the tide is turning from this full-time paradigm to one that pundits and analysts call the "gig economy."

The Transition from FTEs to Gig Workers

Much has been made in the last two years about the gig economy, what it means for workers, and whether it will erode the traditional FTE way working.

For roughly the last half-century, we've seen a transition away from stable employment. The number of people who are self-employed in flexible roles is growing steadily. According to Fast Company, as of May 2015, 15.5 million people in the US were self-employed—an increase of roughly 1 million since May 2014. By 2020, an estimated more than 40 percent of the American workforce, or 60 million people, will be independent workers—freelancers, contractors, and temporary employees.

So as the so-called traditional FTE model gives way to the economy, the prospect is good that, as long as gigging is super-charged by the internet, the gig economy will have an increasing impact on the way people all around the world work.

When Gig Work Was a Way of Life

It turns out that the gigging so many people are talking about and taking part in is a way of life that's not all that different from the way we lived prior to the industrial revolution.

"While it might seem that long-established ways of working are being disrupted, history shows us that the one-person, one-career model is a relatively recent phenomenon," Tawny Paul, a British historian, wrote for Business Insider in July.

"Prior to industrialisation in the 19th century, most people worked multiple jobs to piece together a living. Looking to the past uncovers some of the challenges, benefits and consequences of a gig economy," Paul said.

Paul cited a diary of Edmund Harrold to illustrate the point. "A resident of Manchester in the early 18th century, he was a barber by training and title. He rented a small shop, shaved customers' heads, bought and sold hair, and crafted wigs. In the hours unfilled by this, he worked as a book dealer, and eventually as an auctioneer, selling various items in alehouses within Manchester and in outlying towns. He lent out money when he had it, earning 10% interest on his holdings."

The Internet Propels the Next Wave of Gig Workers

At the turn of the last century, with the rise of the internet, people looking for gigs and those looking to hire flexible workers could connect, seamlessly and efficiently, like never before.

Craigslist, which launched in 1996, provided one of the first global platforms for gigging. It hasn't changed much since—it's a place where people looking for work post their availability free of charge and those looking to hire get what they need for a small cost.

Not long after the emergence of craigslist.org, Web 2.0 and a proliferation of apps ushered in sites highly attuned to the collaborative consumption of the gig economy. TaskRabbit, Lyft, Uber, Thumbtack, Postmates, Dogvacay, Airbnb … the list goes on.

These companies "helped create a novel form of business," as Nathan Heller wrote for the New Yorker in his May 2017 article "Is the Gig Economy Working?"

"The model goes by many names—the sharing economy; the gig economy; the on-demand, peer, or platform economy—but the companies share certain premises. They typically have ratings-based marketplaces and in-app payment systems. They give workers the chance to earn money on their own schedules, rather than through professional accession. And they find toeholds in sclerotic industries," Heller continued.

Sclerotic industries—those that have become rigid and lost the ability to adapt—are ripe for disruption. Think of Uber's disruption of the taxicab industry, based largely on identifying waste and opportunities for innovation in transporting people and now products such as restaurant meals.

More recently, online freelancing platforms that enable consumer and enterprise leaders to connect with virtual workers are taking the gig economy to new heights. Upwork, Contently, PeoplePerHour, Freelance, Fiverr, Amazon's Mechanical Turk and other online freelancing platforms are just a few of these.

Why Some Enterprises Haven't Fully Embraced Gig Workers

Although many enterprises report using flex workers to fulfill some of their business needs, one of the greatest hesitations enterprise leaders have in adopting gig workers is the ability to effectively hire, train and manage them at scale.

That's where companies such as Liveops come in, sourcing a vast network of independent contractor agents who are available to work in customer service and sales. Liveops provides the tools for agent certification on the customer's programs and for monitoring and optimizing agent performance.

This multiplies the power of a flexible workforce, because enterprises no longer have to build their own systems for sourcing, skill development and management of individual gig workers, and they gain access to a network of thousands of virtual agents to handle their business needs on an enterprise scale.

The Gig Economy Is a Result of Larger Changes in the Broader Economy

Clive Hopkins

Clive Hopkins is a journalist and screenwriter. He has written for the Sydney Morning Herald, HRMonthly, BusinessThink, BBC Online, *and the* Guardian.

If the world of work is changing, recruiters need to adapt what they are doing, or risk getting left behind.

Since the global financial crisis, there has been a significant increase in the amount of contract, temporary and freelance work—dubbed "the gig economy"—across Australia and New Zealand.

Understanding the extent of these changes, and why they are happening now, will become a key skill for any successful recruiter.

Not Just Junior Roles

The popular image of the gig economy worker might be the Uber driver, but the trend is finding its way into less expected areas.

Tom Amos, CEO and co-founder at on-demand staffing platform Sidekicker believes the gig economy can extend into a variety of roles, including senior and technical positions.

"The gig economy can be used in a range of roles, whether it is junior admin roles and hospitality right up to highly skilled workers, developers and designers and marketers," he says. "It's also valuable at the executive level—CFOs, CTOs can be really effective on a gig basis as it's an opportunity for organisations to bring in intellectual property (IP) if the business is lacking in a certain area."

This trend is already underway within recruitment sector. "We're placing senior people with experience of working in large

"Understanding the 'gig economy' and the changing world of work," by Clive Hopkins, SEEK Limited. Reprinted by permission.

companies into smaller companies for short periods, in order for the company to absorb their expertise," says Matthew Gribble, Regional Managing Director Michael Page ANZ.

Interestingly, these 'interim executive solutions' are proving to be a disruption, less to permanent work, but more in the management consultancy space. As clients become more aware of the possibility of engaging very high-calibre talent for short time spans, this represents a significant opportunity for recruiters.

Why Is It Happening Now?

"People joining the workforce now have a different mindset from the past," says Andrew Brushfield, Director, Victoria and Western Australia at Robert Half. "People are looking for experiences and growth, and the need for stability is not so ingrained."

Gribble believes the move towards shorter-term roles is also being driven by specialisation.

"Twenty years ago, professionals were generic," he says. "These days, we're demanding more specialist and niche skills. But companies can't employ people with all the niche skills required, as they'd just have too many people."

While the perception of short-term roles may have changed in recent times, Amos argues that the idea of hiring employees for short-term roles isn't new—what's new is how we go about it.

"Previously if you wanted to call a taxi, you'd call a taxi company and if you wanted to buy goods you'd go into a store. What has enabled the gig economy in the format that everyone is now talking about is the rise of technology," he says.

"Technology and its intermediation power has meant that buyers and sellers for hirers and service providers can directly connect."

What Industries Will Be Most Affected?

"All industries are evolving and changing, but the industries most likely to offer project-based work—like tech or creative industries—are most prone to the gig economy," says

Brushfield. "Even Robert Half itself brings in people to work on technical projects."

Of course, some areas of work, such as seasonal agricultural work, have always been and always will be performed on a casual basis. John Harland, Director of ERG Recruitment Group believes that if recruitment firms ignore these less glamorous areas of recruitment, then they do so at their peril.

Limits of the Gig Economy

Harland believes that the gig economy will never replace permanent work, as people will always value the security and longevity that permanent employment can bring. "Permanent employment will continue to thrive where there is a match of company values with that of the employee, and where it's perceived to contribute to their career development and progress."

"When you find a good company, you want to stay with it," he says. "Often after a period of time contracting, people desire that ongoing connection with a culture and this can be limited with contract workers."

Amos believes that the limit of the gig economy comes at the point where expert internal knowledge is paramount for the role. "There is still a huge need for robust full time, part time and casual employment," he says. "The main reason for this is because businesses are crying out for talent and they want to hold onto as much IP as possible.

"I see this workforce as being supplemented by gig workers, who either deal with skills shortages or supply shortages of labour."

The growth of the gig economy also has the potential to impact on the skill levels and career development of workers.

"Of course, contract workers always have the possibility to impress a company to get more work, or even permanent work," says Brushfield.

"If your ambition is to manage large teams of people, the gig economy can serve as a 'between' job," says Gribble. "But employers will assess your success as a manager over perhaps a three year period, rather than three months."

How Can Recruiters Adapt?

"If you know candidates who are happy with this kind of employment, and companies who have these types of needs, then the impact on recruiters is minimal," says Brushfield.

"The challenge for recruiters is having a large enough database, and access to sufficient candidates, to be able to supply niche skill sets with relevant industry experience expediently for specialist roles," says Gribble.

The Future

"Whilst the emerging gig economy is definitely something to be excited about in the future of the workplace, the recruitment sector will always be considered vital in helping candidates find the right job and companies filling their staffing needs," says Brushfield.

"Clients always judge recruiters on the quality of the candidates, as the 'human component' is the most crucial element in recruiting."

Technology Drives the Gig Economy

Dawn Onley

Dawn Onley is a freelance writer based in Washington, DC. She has written for AOL, HR Magazine, *and* Black America Web, *among other publications.*

Workplace experts are having difficulty predicting what is in store for workers of tomorrow. With so many changes happening so quickly, prognosticators say they are unsure about the future of work. At the Future of Work Symposium, sponsored by the Department of Labor in early December, public servants, employers, economists, academics, think tank experts, philanthropists, venture capitalists and labor leaders gathered to brainstorm what employment will look like in the years to come, and to dive into the impact of globalization and technology on the economic landscape of the US.

Hundreds of attendees, panelists and people on social media—all invested in the outcome of the country's job future—took part in the conversation. On one hand, panelists heralded the positive impact technological advancements have made for on-demand jobs, or the gig economy—the workers who work at their own pace and on their own schedule to make money off of what they already own, such as their cars, homes or social media presence. On the other hand, experts and thought leaders say it's hard to regulate these jobs, which typically come without insurance benefits and offer less pay and even less bargaining power.

Most experts foresee an ever-increasing breakdown of the traditional labor market because of the impact of digital technologies. Black and Hispanic workers have felt the greatest impact. According to data from the Bureau of Labor Statistics, while the unemployment rate nationwide for November was 5 percent, the unemployment rate among blacks for that month had increased to 9.4 percent. Hispanics had a 6.4 percent unemployment rate and Asians experienced a 3.9 percent unemployment rate. Even when employed, people who hold jobs as hotel baggage carriers, domestic workers and cooks are increasingly working for subcontractors—which in some cases is a major shift from when these same workers were employed by the hotel or other business and received all of the same benefits that other employees received.

Fixing Disparities

Labor Secretary Thomas E. Perez provided a lesson on the history of work to guide the discussion, while offering perspective on ways to ensure that in the future, workers are protected and valued and that everyone has access to economic prosperity. Perez said the United States has gone from farm to factory to computer-based jobs over hundreds of years and has passed some important laws protecting workers along the way, so it certainly should be able to "find a way to harness new digital technologies in a way that ensures workers are fairly treated and prosperity is broadly shared."

"We can't fall into the trap of believing that the latest innovation is so different and so transformational that we simply can't accommodate and acclimate," Perez said.

"I refuse to shrug my shoulders, throw my hands in the air and say that the degradation of work is the price we pay for smartphones, or that the cost of receiving same-day online purchases is denying someone their basic employment protections," Perez added. "And at the same time, we can't be afraid of technological change. I just as emphatically reject the notion that we have to put the brakes on innovation in order to preserve or advance the dignity of work."

Panel discussions at the three-day symposium explored opportunities and challenges in the changing structure of work, emerging trends, employee benefit coverage, labor standards enforcement, skills training and workforce development.

The conversation delved into the dwindling middle class, a broadening of the working poor, racial and gender pay disparities, and an increased upper class. Most speakers emphasized the need to increase funding so the Bureau of Labor Statistics can conduct and keep more thorough records to help inform future discussion, laws and mandates.

The Gig Economy's Impact

"The structure of the labor market is no longer rewarding workers in the way it used to," said Edward Montgomery, dean of the McCourt School of Public Policy at Georgetown University. "There is a hollowing out of the middle. We're still creating jobs, but we're not creating middle class jobs."

Yet the nature of work is changing, shifting from full-time jobs to contract, freelance and consultation, according to Steven Berkenfeld, a managing director in the Investment Banking Division of Barclays Capital in New York. If a worker is not core to the mission of a company, increasingly, that worker is at risk of losing his or her job. "There's a feeling that technology often does it better, faster [and is] more precise," Berkenfeld said. "I think everyone is affected by technology as a substitute for the workers."

Natalie Foster, fellow with the Institute for the Future in San Francisco, attributed the shift to on-demand and gig jobs to four main reasons:

- People who are in between jobs.
- People looking for supplemental income.
- People searching for flexibility.
- People who are entrepreneurs.

Sarita Gupta, executive director of Jobs with Justice in Washington, D.C., a grassroots network of coalitions and leaders that fight for workers' rights, cautioned that with the increased flexibility of gig work comes some risks as well. "It's less pay; less bargaining power," Gupta said. "Work has become insecure. We need to focus energy on addressing insecure work."

The ones who suffer are the workers, especially certain groups, added Gupta "Large groups of women, workers of color, incarcerated workers—there are so many [impacted] communities out there. When people are struggling to get by, the question on who loses … it's such a moving target."

Path to Enlightenment

Perez thinks meetings like the symposium are getting the right people talking about the challenges and potential solutions. He and thought leaders working to advance workers' rights and opportunities say they can see the path. They're just not completely sure how to get there.

Perez told attendees that the symposium was an "ongoing conversation" that will continue to inform the department's work through the end of the Obama administration and beyond.

"We are actively contemplating what these changes in work will mean for the programs we administer and the laws we enforce," Perez said. "We're figuring out how to adjust what we do, in a way that fulfills our statutory mandate without creating unnecessary impediments to innovation."

With Computers as Bosses, the Gig Economy Shifts Workplace Dynamics

Clark Merrefield

Clark Merrefield is a journalist for Journalist's Resource, *a publication of the Shorenstein Center on Media, Politics and Public Policy at the Harvard Kennedy School. He previously worked as a reporter for the* Daily Beast *and* Newsweek.

I f you work for a boss who has all the emotional intelligence of a computer, consider that someday your boss might actually *be* a computer. That's not a dystopic fantasy—for some workers, it's reality.

Take ridesharing. Millions of cab rides in the US have started with someone pulling out their smartphone, plopping a pin on a map and waiting for a driver to show up and take them on their way. Uber started the mobile ride-hailing revolution a decade ago, and some transportation network company users have probably never called a cab the old fashioned way.

Those who have called for a cab will remember talking to a dispatcher who coordinated their pickup. The dispatcher performed a middle manager function, communicating between drivers and passengers, allocating labor resources according to the company's goals. Then Uber and Lyft came along and automated the dispatcher's job. The automation of leadership isn't likely to stop with the personal transportation revolution, according to a new paper in *Computers in Human Behavior*, which outlines a framework for further explorations into the changing nature of traditional human-to-human workplace hierarchies.

The paper proposes a conceptual framework of computers-as-leaders that can inform research, and a Leadership-TAM, or technology acceptance model. Researchers have used such models to predict "individual adoption and use of technology" and they have been "successfully applied to a broad range of different technologies," the authors write.

Academic theories around automated leadership can help policymakers and the public understand the real consequences of computer bosses, but those theories are lagging behind real-world implementation, according to the paper. The authors assume workers need to perceive their automated leaders as being useful and workers need to be able to interact with automated leaders in an effortless way.

"Technology philosophers say algorithms cannot be leaders because they are not legal persons and they cannot be sanctioned and they don't have inherent moral sentiments and feelings and this is, like, full stop," says social scientist Jenny Wesche, visiting professor at Humboldt University of Berlin and one of the authors. "Although I agree a computer is not a legal person, it's important to be open to this paradigm in order to see the people who are working under the leadership of algorithms. If you say machines cannot be leaders you ignore the people who are already working in such situations."

Computers: From Paperweight to the Corner Office

Researchers typically frame this discussion around what they call "human-computer interaction." When computers first entered workplaces they were viewed as tools. They were much more sophisticated than, say, a hammer. But, like a hammer, an early computer was a mere paperweight if it didn't have a human telling it what to do. "The computer is a moron," Peter Drucker wrote in a classic McKinsey Quarterly essay in 1967.

Around the turn of the 21st century, researchers started to explore computers as team players, with computers and humans acting in cooperation, even as peers. Almost twenty years on, with exponentially greater processing capabilities and artificial learning, the algorithm-as-boss is here for many workers, particularly those in food service and the gig economy.

"Computers are becoming intelligent entities and are already making decisions that seriously influence human work and life," write Wesche and her co-author, University of Fribourg psychologist Andredas Sonderegger.

Major chains in the service sector often use automated scheduling, and so do some hospital systems. A computer, not a shift leader, might tell your favorite barista when to show up in the morning. A few years ago, reporting revealed that the scheduling algorithm Starbucks used was creating havoc for some workers, who were sent scrambling for child care in order to make shifts at odd hours.

"Even if these algorithms maybe are not fully autonomous they nevertheless have a big impact on workers' lives," Wesche says. "It is more drastic in the gig economy because, from my personal view, the workers there are quite exchangeable."

For example, Wesche says that a transportation network company may not be particularly invested in career advancement for drivers who use their smartphone application, "and this is different from most traditional companies, especially in higher-skill jobs."

What's a Leader?

Organizational psychologists have examined from many angles how human leaders and subordinates interact. But when technology is added to the mix, the scholarship tends to focus on how computers can help human leaders and teams—less so the idea of computers as, "active agents in leadership and team processes," the authors write.

Some researchers put personal management styles—charismatic or inspirational, for example—at the core of being a leader. Leadership is, "a shared human process," workplace researchers Wilfred Drath and Charles Palus wrote in the mid-1990s. Other definitions of leadership, like that put forward by University of Albany psychologist Gary Yukl, are more functional and have to do with one individual guiding another in structuring activities and relationships. Workers with bosses who primarily do things that can be quantified—scheduling, establishing goals and priorities, monitoring job performance—are those seemingly likely to encounter automated leaders.

"I think we will also in traditional companies see increasingly that functions will be automated, because it is much more efficient," says Wesche. "But the question is, how do we design it?"

That design may need to account for some lost human element. Social exchange theory observes that workplace relationships can become something more than a financial transactional. Professional relationships can develop beyond an employee being productive for an organization in exchange for monetary or other compensation. Mutual trust between people builds over time, and this can play out in positive social ways. If a barista's grandmother dies their longtime boss might empathize, approve time off without a fuss, and trust the employee will be back to work when they're ready — and, perhaps, be open to taking an early shift in a pinch.

"It's important to do research on the way that humans, with their need for social contact, can interact with a computer leader so that they can in fact flourish at work, they can perform well and at the same time develop personally and experience well-being," Wesche says.

Hey Alexa, How's My TPS Report?

Humans are arguably already quite comfortable interacting, at least on a basic level, with non-anthropomorphic algorithms. A growing body of research, for example, is exploring how adults and children interact with smart speakers. Alexa, the voice of the Amazon Echo, is backed by sophisticated algorithms and it reverberates from a body that has zero resemblance to the human form—but people can still form real connections with it.

"So my daughter thinks she knows Alexa's habits and she can understand Alexa even if I can't," one parent recounted in 2017 conference paper that analyzed 278,000 Alexa commands.

"It's kind of creepy. As I say it out loud it's totally weird that my daughter is friends with a tower that sits on my counter."

Advanced economies are complex and some workers may never interact, at least directly, with an automated leader. For them, the concept of computers-as-bosses may be moot. But for others, like gig workers and food service staff, the future is now—and there are still a lot of unknowns as to how automated leaders might change the lives of their human charges.

"It's not the question of whether this future will come, or whether functions can be automated, or whether artificial intelligence is taking over more and more functions at work—it's a question of how it's going to happen," Wesche says. "We should be aware of that. I think it is the responsibility of scientists and journalists and politicians to guide this development and set boundaries and discuss standards and discuss development—and not so much discuss whether it is going to come or not."

The Gig Economy Does Not Have a Serious Impact on Most Traditional Work

Greg Rosalksy

Greg Rosalksy is a writer and reporter at NPR's Planet Money, *a podcast and blog focused on explaining economic issues.*

I n recent months, a slew of studies has debunked predictions that we're witnessing the dawn of a new "gig economy." The US Bureau of Labor Statistics (BLS) found that there was actually a *decline* in the categories of jobs associated with the gig economy between 2005 and 2017. Larry Katz and the late Alan Krueger then revised their influential study that had originally found gig work was exploding. Instead, they found it had only grown modestly. Other economists ended up finding the same—and now writers are declaring the gig economy is "a big nothingburger."

The Gig Revolution's True Believer

Arun Sundararajan, a professor at the NYU Stern School of Business and the author of *The Sharing Economy: The End of Employment and the Rise of Crowd-Based Capitalism*, remains a true believer in the gig revolution. Sundararajan has been pushing the idea that the gig economy—and specifically work done through digital platforms like Uber and Airbnb—will conquer traditional employment. Instead of an economy dominated by big corporations, he believes it will be dominated by "a crowd" of self-employed entrepreneurs and workers transacting with customers through digital platforms. "We are in the early days of a fundamental reorganization of the economy," Sundararajan said while riding to the airport in, naturally, an Uber.

When asked about the onslaught of data contradicting his thesis, Sundararajan said the Bureau of Labor Statistics continues "to underestimate the size of the gig economy and in particular of the platform-based gig economy." The best BLS estimate of the number of gig workers employed through digital platforms—whether full-time, part-time or occasionally—is one percent of the total US workforce, or about 1.6 million workers, as of mid-2017. Sundararajan argues that the survey questions the BLS used to gather this data were clunky and don't quite capture what's going on.

While Sundararajan disagrees with estimates about the size of the gig economy, he agrees that most people doing new gig work are either Uber and Lyft drivers or Airbnb hosts. It's no coincidence that housing and transportation have been the two main areas of growth. Homes and cars are the most valuable things many people possess, and the Internet and smartphones have made using them to make extra money much easier. Sundararajan makes a good case that there will be growth in areas like health care and accounting as well, but there is little evidence to suggest we're witnessing "the end of employment."

The Resilience of Traditional Employment

Employment as we know it is a relatively new development. At the turn of the 20th century, almost half of Americans were still self-employed as farmers and ranchers and artisans. But in the background, a mighty organization called the company was taking off. By 1960, around 85% of Americans were employees of companies.

While Sundararajan believes our economy will once again be dominated by the self-employed, he admits that full-time employment has "tons of advantages." It offers stability, a steady paycheck, and benefits. We've collectively engineered much of our social safety net around participating in this system. All of this means, Sundararajan says, "we're going to see full-time employment remain resilient, even though there are more efficient ways of organizing economic activity." He believes work done through gig platforms can be more efficient than work done in a traditional company—and that will spell the company's doom.

The Mysterious Benefits of the Firm

Economists were long confused by the existence of companies. They celebrated prices and competition—and it seemed natural that the most efficient way to do business was as individuals transacting within the open market. Need an advertiser? Hire one for a few weeks. Want design work? Work for the highest bidder until the project is done.

From this traditional view, it seemed odd that we would organize ourselves as full-time employees in top-down, bureaucratic organizations insulated from the market. Then came Ronald Coase, who won a Nobel Prize in 1991 in large part because of his 1937 paper, "The Nature of The Firm." Coase argued that the reason firms exist is that it's costly for individuals to transact in the market. You have to search for trustworthy people with quality goods or services and then haggle with them, and doing this over and over is inefficient. Within a company, Coase argued, these "transaction costs" are minimized. You can quickly walk to your colleague's desk and share ideas without having to figure out if they're shady. You can share resources, tools, and machinery. You can work in a team and specialize in different tasks. And you can do this all without having to continually negotiate over the price of everything.

The dawn of a new gig economy has seemed plausible because the Internet has been dramatically reducing transaction costs. Search engines have made it incredibly cheap to find goods and services, compare prices, and get bargains. Social media and peer reviews have made it easier to determine if people are trustworthy. E-commerce has made it easier to process payments. You can click a button on a mobile phone and instantaneously have GPS guide drivers right to you. But as big as these efficiency gains have been, a new economy based on crowds of people doing gigs through digital platforms—as exciting or scary as that might sound—still doesn't compare to one based on the efficiencies and stability of the good old-fashioned company.

The Traditional Economy Remains the Best Bet for Businesses

David Marin-Guzman

David Marin-Guzman is a workplace correspondent with the Australian Financial Review *whose writing focuses on industrial relations, workplace, policy, and leadership from Sydney.*

Reports of the death of traditional employment have been much exaggerated.

That's the takeaway from a growing chorus of economists and experts who dispute predictions the gig economy would change everything.

We were told the workforce would be transformed into a mass of freelancers, agile smaller firms would capitalise on this shift—superseding large companies—and governments would have to deal with diminishing income tax revenues and superannuation contributions.

But it's now five years since the likes of Uber and Airtasker popularised the concept of the gig economy and so far the doom and gloom forecasts have proved wide of the mark.

It appears the more things change, the more they stay the same.

In a conference paper delivered this week, Griffith University Professor David Peetz, a former deputy department head of industrial relations in the Keating government, analysed ABS stats and found self-employment is falling, full-time employment is increasing, and casualisation has been "pretty much stable" for the past decade.

"The death of employment is an international myth without international substance," he said.

The platform economy may be the biggest threat to the standard employment model, "but it's not dead yet, and likely never will be".

"Why the gig economy hasn't taken your job," by David Marin-Guzman, The Australian Financial Review, July 27, 2018. Reprinted by permission.

Traditional employment is still the preferred model for work, Peetz says, because it still offers business huge advantages—and remains the best means of control.

No Rise in Contractors Since 2012

The latest ABS data shows independent contractors, which is how most gig workers would be classified, has not changed as a proportion of the workforce since 2012.

While there are more individuals who classify themselves as contractors, they still account for less than 11 per cent of workers.

As for tax revenue, the parliamentary budget office found in a report released this month that the gig economy was yet to have an impact.

The government had been concerned the shift to a peer-to-peer economy, where more workers would be self-employed, threatened reductions in income tax revenue and an expansion of the black economy.

But, as of 2017 at any rate, this had not occurred.

The proportion of individuals who identify as self-employed in their main job had not increased and, also, salaries and wages as a share of GDP had not experienced a sustained fall.

"Although the many disruptions taking place in the labour market will undoubtedly lead to challenges, the current data does not reveal the negative implications for the personal income tax base so far," the report concluded.

Despite predictions the labour market shift would see the decline in importance of larger companies, firm size is not decreasing. Businesses with 200 or more employees accounted for about 24 per cent of private sector employees in 2014-15, similar to 2009-10.

For their part, gig companies insist things are still on the up and up.

Online consulting platform Expert360, which counts more than 19,000 freelancers, says it's seeing an influx of sign ups. It maintains much of the growth in the gig economy is coming from the white-collar workforce.

And the online job marketplace, Airtasker, has more than 2.3 million members who perform $100 million worth of tasks each year.

Unions Exaggerating the Problem

The Australian Council of Trade Unions says these companies have contributed to an "explosion in insecure work" and that it's worse now than it was a generation ago.

The union peak body has made "insecure" work a centrepiece of its industrial relations campaign ahead of the next federal election, calling for a legislative crackdown on casuals, labour hire and the gig economy.

But Australian Industry Group chief executive Innes Willox says the union movement is exaggerating the problem.

"The unions in Australia have been scaremongering about the demise of permanent employment for the past 25 years, but there is no sign their predictions will come true," he said.

"Businesses need to attract and retain skilled and dedicated employees, and it is easier to do this with permanent employment arrangements."

While casual employment increased in the 1980s and 1990s, it has hovered around 25 per cent of the workforce, including self-employed, for the past decade.

Australian Institute economist for the Centre of Future Work, Jim Stanford counters that while casual employment has been higher in the past, it is still "near record highs" and has increased from a low of 23.5 per cent in 2012.

He agrees self-employment has not grown as a proportion of the workforce but argues "insecurity" within that class of work is more acute.

From 2012 to 2017, self-employed workers working less than full-time hours has risen from 32 per cent to 35 per cent.

Fissuring of the Workplace

UTS Business School associate professor Sarah Kaine says it is too early to tell the impact of the gig economy.

She argues Uber drivers and Deliveroo riders, referred to as "partners" or "team members," may not be showing up in the data because they don't know whether to classify themselves as contractors or business owners.

While Peetz maintains traditional employment is still unlikely to be affected, he and Kaine agree that there has been a "fissuring" of the workplace in certain sectors such as fast-food, mining and cleaning.

These sectors distance themselves from employees through franchising, labour hire and contracting in a bid to disperse risk through organisations.

In many cases, engaging a peripheral workforce is legitimate, such as when a business is not prepared to hire people in case of a business downturn.

But it also raises issues of responsibility and how the core business can control and influence workers.

Kaine says this is where Uber and other gig platforms come in, using technology and algorithms to develop "a new frontier of control."

Whether it be surge pricing for peak periods or customer star ratings that act as performance management, the gig economy is introducing new levers for business to influence behaviour when they have an "arms-length" relationship to their workforce.

But for many organisations it appears this model is still too experimental, involving too much risk and uncertainty.

"It may be that it requires too much thought from organisations," Kaine says.

"In the end, it's much easier to have people in-house, at least casual, that you can employ with well established mechanisms of control and motivation."

Gig Work Is Usually Just a Temporary Option for Workers

Adewale Maye

Adewale Maye is a research assistant at the Center for Law and Social Policy (CLASP). He was previously an intern at the Center for Economic and Policy Research (CEPR).

S ocial networks and the development of platform technologies have drastically transformed the way people live, work, and spend their money. The use of information and communication technologies has become an important aspect of jobs in occupations ranging from medical assistants to fast food operators, lawyers, steel workers, and others employed in traditional employment relations. The growth and popularity of online and app-based platforms like Uber, GrubHub, and TaskRabbit have raised the profile of the gig economy and created the impression that employer-less work and gig jobs are a pervasive aspect of modern employment. A lack of consistent, rigorous data on twenty-first-century employment relations allowed speculation about the role of independent contractors, and especially gig workers, to dominate conversations about the future of work.

Predictions of the rise and dominance of the gig economy led many observers to fear these types of jobs would supplant traditional employment relations and leave many workers without the protections of minimum wage, overtime pay, family and medical leave, employer-provided vacation, or pension benefits. A 2015 study by economists Alan Krueger of Princeton and Larry Katz of Harvard provided academic support for the predicted shift of workers from traditional to alternative work arrangements. They found that between 2005 and 2015 the share of independent contractors in total employment rose by an impressive five percentage points, from 10.7 percent to 15.8 percent, and attributed much of the increase to gig jobs with Uber, Lyft, and similar companies. They also reported that 95 percent of all job growth over that period was in gig jobs, further fueling the belief that the gig economy holds the key to the future of work.

In May 2017, the Bureau of Labor Statistics (BLS) repeated its contingent worker survey (CWS) — a rigorous and systematic repeat of its 2005 and earlier surveys. In contrast to the Katz and Kreuger study, the CWS found that, as in 2005, nine-in-ten workers held a main job characterized by traditional employer–employee work arrangements. The CWS found no increase in the share of independent contractors in total employment over the 12 years from 2005 to 2017. And, it found that just 1.0 percent of workers held a gig economy job either as their main job, second job, or to make additional income. A study by JPMorgan Chase that tracked earnings of 39 million Chase checking account holders found that between October 2012 and March 2018, just 1.1 percent of the sample of account holders included a worker with earnings from an online platform, 1.0 percent from transportation platforms, and 0.1 from other employment platforms.

The disconnect between speculation about the prevalence and threat of gig jobs and the reality of how many workers actually held such jobs can be seen in the number of Google searches for 'gig economy' over the last four years compared to the monthly changes in share of employment in select sectors of the gig economy between 2013 and 2018.

The term gig economy has seen a steady growth in Google searches over the last four years, punctuated by occasional surges. The first two dramatic increases in gig economy Google searches began in mid-2015 to late-2016 coinciding with the release of the study from Katz and Krueger. The rise in searches thereafter reflects the reception of the study and the dominance of the gig economy in discussions about the future of work. In contrast, The data on the changes in share of employment in the gig economy shows that the share of workers that participated in transportation and non-transport work platforms has seen very little growth over the past four years, with employment in both sectors reaching only 1.0 or 1.1 percent in the BLS and JPMorgan Chase studies.

Katz and Kreuger have now walked back their earlier results. In a new paper released in January 2019, they note that what they thought was a trend of rapidly increasing gig jobs was actually a blip, due to the slow recovery from the recession and financial crisis of the 2007–2008 period. Many workers used short-term, freelance, and contingent work to fill the gap in income. This was a stopgap for working families, rather than a trend in employment; workers turned to standard jobs as the economy improved and these jobs became plentiful again. As for the scare statistic that 95 percent of net new jobs created over that period went to independent contractors, the 2005–2015 period saw widespread job losses in many sectors of the economy so that any sector that created jobs (i.e., health care) would have accounted for the lion's share of net job creation. By 2017, it was clear that employment growth was mainly in standard work arrangements, which increased its share of employment slightly compared with 2005, while the share of independent contractors in employment declined slightly over the 2005–2017 time period.

While the data show that the traditional world of work won't be disappearing anytime soon, the questionable speculations about the gig economy that have a hold on popular imagination and on policy discussions is also not likely to soon dissipate.

Gig Work Has Long Had a Place in the Economy

Tawny Paul

Tawny Paul is a senior lecturer in economic and social history at the University of Exeter in the United Kingdom. Her research focuses on gender and the social history of debt, particularly in eighteenth-century Britain.

The Taylor Report, the UK government's recent major review of modern work, paid particular attention to the "gig economy." This is the idea that the traditional model of work—where people often have a clear career progression and a job for life—has been upended. It encompasses "self-employed" Uber drivers to the web developer freelancers and it allows workers more freedom—but also denies them benefits and protective regulation.

While it might seem that long-established ways of working are being disrupted, history shows us that the one person, one career model is a relatively recent phenomenon. Prior to industrialisation in the 19th century, most people worked multiple jobs to piece together a living. Looking to the past uncovers some of the challenges, benefits and consequences of a gig economy.

The diaries of three men in 18th-century Britain that I have found give a fascinating insight into how middle class people—the supposed beneficiaries of today's gig economy—made multiple employments work. Edmund Harrold, a resident of Manchester in the early 18th century was a barber by training and title. He rented a small shop, shaved customers' heads, bought and sold hair, and crafted wigs. In the hours unfilled by this he worked as a book dealer, and eventually as an auctioneer, selling various items in alehouses within Manchester and in outlying towns. He lent out money when he had it, earning 10% interest on his holdings.

Another enthusiastic embracer of the gig economy was Thomas Parsons, working as a stone carver in the city of Bath in 1769, as well as an amateur scientist—work that we might normally classify as leisure. In the West Country, John Cannon took jobs as an agricultural labourer, excise man, failed maltster, and teacher.

Like people earning money through the gig economy today, the three men were thrown into a world of precariousness. They had independence but fretted frequently about having enough money to pay bills, and feared the potential for failure. Parsons agonised about his ability to pay his debts, noting in one entry:

> Am in debt and know not how to pay. This gives me great uneasiness—what a multiplicity of concerns have I to employ my thoughts!

In one entry, Harrold thanked God for "tolerable business" and noted that he lived very comfortably. By the next month, he would write that he was "ill set for money," that he had very little work, and described being "in great straite what to do."

All three diarists earned a comfortable, though modest subsistence for tradesmen of the time, earning between £50 and £70 a year, which made them part of the growing middle class in terms of income. But in an economy of multiple jobs, their income was precarious, and this had a big impact on their lives. Cannon described himself as the "tennis ball of fortune."

More Than the Money

Money was a concern, but the diaries make clear that, like today, work was also about more than pay. The experiences of these three men show that people chose their work because different jobs offered different forms of fulfilment. Some tasks earned them money, but other roles gave them social status. In some cases, they even judged fulfilment and the status these jobs gave them as highly as material gain.

The opportunity for networking, building reputations and power could be equally as important as the cash earned. In fact, the value of work in terms of status and income could have an inverse relationship. Parsons made most of his money from his stone-cutting business rather than his intellectual pursuits, but it was his scientific experimentation that conferred the most status. That status, in turn, helped him get contracts.

Historical accounts of the gig economy remind us that we need to think about work as more than a form of wage earning, but as something crucial to our social and cultural lives. We define ourselves according to the jobs that we do. Though the recently-released Taylor review of Britain's gig economy focuses on wages, benefits, and regulation, it also clearly recognises work as an experience. The report is peppered with words like "happiness" and "aspiration."

Plus, we might notice that work—even gig work—depends upon status. Today, workers relying on online platforms for work depend upon their user rating. Status and employment go hand-in-hand. And activities that help a person build status blur the distinctions between work and leisure, or unpaid and paid work. Work, for men like Parsons, Harrold and Cannon, was a social practice. It was not only a productive activity to support themselves, but was rather an undertaking that established skill, independence and self-worth.

What Counts as Work?

The gig economy considered in a historical context challenges us to better define the simple category of "work." Should we define work as tasks undertaken for pay? Or should we include productive labour that is not paid?

Harrold was the nominal breadwinner of his family, but the household also depended upon his wife's work. Sarah rented a room in their house to lodgers, sold secondhand clothing and washed other people's clothes. For these tasks, she earned money. But like many women in the 18th century (and today), much of Sarah's work was unpaid. She cared for children, baked bread, and brewed ale. These tasks sustained the household and its reproduction, but because they were unpaid, they remain unrecognised as work. Even though she spent her days working, Sarah would have been listed as having no occupation in formal tax or census records.

In today's gig economy, more and more informal domestic tasks are becoming forms of paid work. Will accounting for these help us to better recognise the invisible work that takes place in the household?

The gig economy certainly poses challenges to the well-being of workers. The disruption that it brings, however, offers an opportunity to better account for the diversity of different kinds of work that take place in society, and to recognise the people who perform it.

Organizations to Contact

The editors have compiled the following list of organizations concerned with the issues debated in this book. The descriptions are derived from materials provided by the organizations. All have publications or information available for interested readers. This list was compiled on the date of publication of the present volume; the information provided here may change. Be aware that many organizations take several weeks or longer to respond to inquiries, so allow as much time as possible.

American Economic Association (AEA)
2014 Broadway Suite 305
Nashville, TN 37203
phone: (615) 322-2595
website: www.aeaweb.org

The AEA is a nonpartisan, nonprofit organization that publishes and analyzes economic research. The organization publishes multiple journals related to economics, as well as resources for economists, students, and the public.

The Brookings Institution
1775 Massachusetts Avenue NW
Washington, DC 20036
phone: (202) 797-6000
email: communications@brookings.edu
website: www.brookings.edu

The Brookings Institution is a nonprofit public policy organization that conducts independent research. The Brookings Institution uses its research to provide recommendations that advance the goals of strengthening American democracy, fostering social welfare and security, and securing a cooperative international system. The organization publishes a variety of books, reports, and commentary.